WHY
GOOD
PEOPLE
DO BAD
THINGS

ALSO BY BRUCE HAMSTRA

*How Therapists Diagnose: Seeing Through
the Psychiatric Eye*

WHY GOOD PEOPLE DO BAD THINGS

HOW TO MAKE MORAL CHOICES IN AN IMMORAL WORLD

BRUCE HAMSTRA, Ed.D.

A Birch Lane Press Book
Published by Carol Publishing Group

To my mother,
Dora M. Koller,
and the memory of my grandmother,
Leona M. Neal

A Birch Lane Press Book
Published by Carol Publishing Group
Birch Lane Press is a registered trademark of Carol Communications, Inc.

Editorial Offices: 600 Madison Avenue, New York, N.Y. 10022
Sales and Distribution Offices: 120 Enterprise Avenue, Secaucus, N.J. 07094
In Canada: Canadian Manda Group, One Atlantic Avenue, Suite 105, Toronto,
    Ontario M6K 3E7
Queries regarding rights and permissions should be addressed to
Carol Publishing Group, 600 Madison Avenue, New York, N.Y. 10022

Carol Publishing Group books are available at special discounts for bulk
purchases, sales promotion, fund-raising, or educational purposes.
Special editions can be created to specifications. For details, contact:
Special Sales Department, Carol Publishing Group, 120 Enterprise Avenue,
Secaucus, N.J. 07094.

Manufactured in the United States of America
10 9 8 7 6 5 4 3 2 1

Library of Congress Cataloging-in-Publication Data

Hamstra, Bruce
    Why good people do bad things : how to make moral choices in an
    immoral world / Bruce Hamstra.
        p.   cm.
    "A Birch Lane Press book."
    ISBN 1–55972–324–6
    1. Decision-making (Ethics).   I. Title.
BJ1419.H36   1995
170—dc20   95-19227
                                                                CIP

CONTENTS

BENCHMARKS

PREFACE

Why Good People Do Bad Things explores our heroic struggles to be kind, fair, empathetic, and responsible while under siege from the fascinating, often startling whirlwinds of self-deception, psychic distortion, and social influence. It's about our lifelong challenge to do the right thing, how we unwittingly lose our way in the process, and how we can get back on track without compromising common sense and logic. It's about the joy and power of rediscovering the good person within.

My goal in writing this book was to provide a practical, down-to-earth, reasonable guide for personal exploration. Although not written in an academic manner, the observations are drawn from important research in psychology, moral development, and ethics. My intent was to clarify the practical link between personal psychology, group psychology, moral development, our quest for meaning, and the ethical dilemmas that we witness and grapple with every day. For example:

- Like most people, Susan describes herself as a good person. She goes out of her way to help others. But to land her first major job as a radio disc jockey, she fabricated half her resume. "Everyone does it. It would be stupid not to. How else would I get their attention? If you told the truth in this business, you'd get nowhere. Even the bosses lie." Does this woman have a psychological problem, a "weak" moral character, or what?

- At age sixteen, Larry is a very talented musician, a good student, and a loving son. Larry shot and killed an eighteen-year-old Vietnamese neighbor. "He was messing with my girlfriend and put me down. The guy wouldn't listen. I thought he was looking to blow me away. What else could I do?" Larry's family and friends are in shock. "Such a good kid. How could he do such a thing?" Larry still believes he did the right thing.

• Sheila, a mail carrier, murdered both of her young children because "the new guy I loved didn't want to get involved with some other man's kids." How could she kill her own kids? Is she crazy? Is she just plain evil? Do her actions even merit "understanding"?

• A faithful husband and loving father, Matt wrote a marketing plan that unloaded watered-down baby formula to Third World countries. "It really didn't hurt anybody. We told the distributors about the manufacturing error and gave them a huge price break, which they passed on to consumers. It would have been a sin to throw it all away when people are starving. Besides, I had little choice in the matter. My boss made that perfectly clear." So what is Matt *really* like, anyway?

• Connie seduced her more-than-willing boss to further her career. Afterward, she was overwhelmed by guilt. Her therapist and a lawyer convinced her that she was really the victim of sexual harassment. Connie filed suit. Was Connie wrong?

• Theodore has had multiple affairs, yet he claims to love his wife more than anything else in the world. "I can't bear to hurt her, but I do it all the time. It's like I'm suddenly invaded by lustful little demons that overwhelm my sensibilities. Anne says it's plain and simple: If I loved her enough, I'd resist them. She can't seem to understand my dilemma."

PRACTICAL GUIDELINES, IMMENSE REWARDS

How do we sort through and make sense of actions and dilemmas like these? And when they affect us personally—at home, at work, or in our relationships—how do we know what's really going on? Are we or those we love suffering from lapses in conscience, poor judgment, flaws of character, or psychological hangups? Where does our personal responsibility begin and end? Furthermore, what can we do about it?

In the larger dimensions, why do so many of us still experience a disturbing sense of emptiness and lack of fulfillment, even though our psyches have been analyzed to the hilt? It feels as if something has been lost, but we're not quite sure what it is. What are we looking for, and how can we get it back?

In *Why Good People Do Bad Things*, you will learn:

• How to view your character, your actions, and your life from a refreshing new perspective.

• How to identify, balance, and breathe life into your personal values; how they get out of whack.

• What morality is all about, and why it doesn't have to be a suffocating list of dos and don'ts. Use it with reason to enrich your life and feel better about yourself.

• The best ways to nurture empathy, moral reasoning, and sensitivity. Learn how parenting styles may affect a child's budding conscience.

• How we all fool ourselves with blind spots, excuses, unconscious defenses, and other psychological shenanigans. Learn to identify traps and pitfalls.

• Important tips for sorting through and making difficult ethical decisions.

• The qualities of character that will empower your actions.

• How to break through the clouds of shame, guilt, and fear that obscure the good person within.

This sounds like a very tall order. But it really doesn't need to be a complicated, overwhelming process. You don't need to be a moral philosopher, psychologist, theologian, saint, or martyr to understand and apply these important principles to your life. Nor do you have to subscribe to a particular faith or belief. As you will see, they simply make good sense.

ACKNOWLEDGMENTS

Given the complex, encompassing nature of this fascinating topic, which delves into the mysteries of our capacity for good and bad, it would have been easy and relatively safe to rest on personal perspectives, beliefs, and nebulous philosophical arguments. To do so, however, would have violated the reader's trust and turned a blind eye to the efforts of those who have dedicated their professional lives to the study of moral development and psychology. Although I have not interrupted the text with academic citations, the influence of these individuals has been immense.

In particular, I would like to express gratitude to the following researchers and writers, whose works have challenged and expanded the narrow bounds of personal belief and opinion: Joseph Reimer (Brandeis University, formerly of Boston University, where he sparked my initial interest in moral development), James Rest (University of Minnesota), William Damon (Brown University), Anne Colby (Radcliffe College), Michael Schulman and Eva Mekler (psychologists and authors), Thomas Lickona (State University of New York, Cortland), Mary Nicholas (Yale University), Ervin Staub (University of Massachusetts, Amherst), Kent Hodgson (business consultant and trainer, Hodgson and Associates), C. R. Snyder (University of Kansas), and Roy Baumeister (Case Western Reserve University).

My thanks, once again, to my superb agent, Jane Dystel, who persisted in spite of several false starts as the project evolved. Her commitment has been greatly appreciated. Hillel Black, my editor at Birch Lane Press, has been an absolute joy. His steady hand, depth of knowledge, sense of humor, and broad perspective have been an experience in and of itself.

Close to the heart, I would like to thank my brother, Roger Hamstra, and my life-long friend, Max Randall Martin, whose enduring quests for larger perspectives have been inspirational and challenging. Love and gratitude to my wife, Marsha Medalie, who is the center, B. W. Binswanger, the ever-present lapcat, and Vivian Medalie, the best mother-in-law.

Finally, in writing about concepts of morality, there is always a risk of being seen in a particularly uncomfortable, artificial light. To dispel any misconceptions, I would also like to dedicate this book to those whom I have unfairly hurt, through indifference, callousness, selfishness, or ignorance.

PART I

GOOD PEOPLE, BAD DEEDS:
GETTING LOST

ONE

Getting Hurt, Hurting Others:
Searching for the Right Thing to Do

You *know* how it feels, even if this isn't a picture of *your* life:

> "My husband rolled in drunk again last night, blowing off our anniversary. I don't know what to think. I'm angry and hurt, but then again, what if it's really a disease? How much can I hold him responsible? My mother-in-law says I'm partially to blame. She calls me an enabler. Is this just an excuse for her son?"

> "I know for a fact that my best friend's wife is having an affair. Should I tell him? What's the right thing to do?"

> "My young nephew lies and steals and doesn't seem to have regard or respect for anything. How did he get that way? Does he need a stern hand and lectures about right and wrong values, or does he have some sort of psychological problem?"

> "There are so many things that I can't say to my father. Every time I see him, the unspoken words eat little holes in my stomach. He's so smug and unrepentant. Why didn't I confront him years ago when it happened? Maybe I'm partially to blame. Is it too late? Should I just forgive and forget?"

"My boss has given me an ultimatum: find a way to hide the extent of last year's losses or I'm gone. What a gutless creep! He can't even take responsibility for his own mismanagement. Should I blow the whistle? Who cares, anyhow? And if he fires me, should I sue him?"

"It's beyond my comprehension. How could he have done it? Innocent people, children, maimed and killed by his bomb. I thought my neighbor was just a good, decent guy. Sure, he ranted on about big government and the erosion of personal liberty, but I didn't think he was some crazed terrorist. Why didn't I see it and do something? I thought it was innocent talk."

"I watch the daily slaughter on the news and I can't even cry anymore. Is this how people really are, underneath it all?"

"There are so many things I've done that I'm truly sorry for. I'm not sure why they happened. I feel that I'm basically a good person but something has gotten lost along the way. Why does my life feel as if it doesn't have any direction? Is there something missing, or is this how all people feel?"

LOOKING FOR SOMETHING MORE

Does the inner dialogue sound familiar? Most of us have had similar thoughts and feelings. This is the mundane stuff of daily existence, yet it can be enough to drive anyone up a wall. How do you deal with it? If you turn to a psychotherapist for help, you could get a lot of evasive answers related to your lack of self-esteem or your tendency to avoid your "real" feelings. True, you can use the normal tools of psychology to gain some important insights about yourself and others, but when it comes to making a few decisions about the best thing to do, you may be left high and dry. In fact, most of our important life decisions go far beyond the limits of individual psychology.

Turning to a minister, preacher, or rabbi, you may be asked to accept a particular view of the world and to base your decisions strictly on faith or tradition. While this kind of guidance is a powerful, vital resource for many people, what if you don't believe in God, heaven, hell, or anything remotely religious? Even if you're an atheist, you're still faced with decisions about doing the right thing. Turn to your lawyer and you're likely to drown in paperwork, ambiguous legal interpretations, and a swamp of bills. Thanks a lot, but no thanks. Legal technicalities don't always reflect the right thing to do.

Looking closely at the issues involved, you may agree that it's difficult to separate out all the elements lurking behind each dilemma. Most of these dilemmas, in addition to the usual psychological dynamics, center on:

- the right and wrong of hurting others and being hurt;
- blame and responsibility;
- forgiveness;
- personal goodness and becoming a better person;
- doing the right thing;
- figuring out how people bring themselves to do the awful things they do; and
- the goodness of human nature in general.

We are faced with issues like this every day. Many are fraught with moral implications and consequences, although we may not view them in that light. Most of us are wary and distrustful of words like "morality," particularly someone else's version of it. Rightly so. We know all too well how the concept has been used and abused in the past. But, like it or not, *we enter the realm of morality whenever our actions might harm (or help) others.* Ignoring this fact doesn't make it go away, and leaves us stranded in a maze of indecision and bewilderment. As you will see, closing our eyes to morality also undermines our emotional well-being, the quality of our relationships, and the richness of our lives.

So, given our distrust and skepticism, where might we turn? Much of the answer lies in a powerful brew that's been fermenting for years, a mixture so potent that many of us have been afraid to taste it for fear of losing our objectivity. I'm referring here to a mixture of psychology, moral philosophy, and ethics. Most people will add a healthy dose of religion and spirituality for meaning, stability, guidance, and depth, but that's a personal choice.

Wait a minute, you say, haven't we been down that road before? Remember the Inquisition, the Salem witch trials, and the Holocaust? Objectivity was wiped out by a flood of beliefs—and moral philosophy, with or without religion, was used to justify all sorts of atrocities. Aren't we talking about a dangerous brew here?

Absolutely! But let's not kid ourselves. Psychology and morality have always swirled in the same pot. Siphoning off one without the other has serious limitations. Too many questions remain unanswered. Reducing the human psyche to an oozing heap of psychological defenses and brain chemicals may be convenient and safe, but it avoids the larger issues of living that we must all face. It also deprives us of extremely valuable tools and guidelines for personal enrichment and understanding.

So how do you drink of this brew without falling prey to its demons? How do you keep a clear head? That's the subject of this book. To see how this is done, as well as what can go wrong, we'll follow the moral lives of a small cast of characters. The primary players are Eric and Vanessa, who are stuck in an abusive relationship; David and Shana, who are involved in a tempestuous affair; Noreen, David's loving wife; Richard, their son, who is failing in college; Zachary, a moralistic con man; Jennifer, a pregnant fifteen-year-old caught up with an older boyfriend and his group; and Elaine, who faces a major ethical dilemma at work.

Their stories are unique and personal but the principles underlying their dilemmas are universal. You could find them running throughout your own life. To get an in-depth view of all the forces at work in our characters' lives, each chapter will address a different aspect of their moral and psychological being, as well as other important issues. You will see how their dilemmas play out as the chapters progress. Other case examples will be explored along the way. In this chapter you will see how moral and psychological ingredients surface in real life and how they act as catalysts for each other. Neither acts in a vacuum.

GETTING THE BIGGER PICTURE

Vanessa is a striking twenty-four-year-old woman with bright auburn hair, radiant blue eyes, and an ominous-looking bruise shaped like a crescent moon running from behind her left ear, across her left cheek, and down to her chin. An inadvertent smile triggers a grimace, a painful edge her makeup can't soften. She is trained as a dental hygienist, but stopped working two years ago after her son, Eddie, was born. Eric, her husband of three years, is struggling to make ends meet as the assistant manager of a large sporting goods store. Vanessa remains very much in love with Eric, although she is frightened by her dependency on a man who repeatedly lashes out in rage, then begs for forgiveness. She is plagued by flashbacks of Eric towering over her twisted body, clumps of auburn hair in his fists.

> Sometimes I feel so bad for Eric. He's just like a little boy, really, a twenty-six-year-old boy. He needs a lot of love, kindness, and understanding to get over some

of the awful things he went through as a kid. It's a difficult process, but he's slowly learning from our love. Deep down inside, he's a really good guy, but he needs my help bringing it out. I know he doesn't mean to hurt me, but the frustrations of his job, coupled with the stress of being a new father, drive him to the breaking point. I can understand that. Also, I can be a real bitch at times. Like he says, a typical, demanding female.

Money is a problem, particularly for me. When he's in one of his rages, he accuses me of diddling our money away, which simply isn't true. The baby needs certain things and so do I. His reaction has been to cut back on my "allowance." But then he'll turn around and buy me something wonderful. He's like that, so unpredictable.

Eric has only smacked Eddie's behind a couple of times. I don't think he'll ever lose control with him. Besides, Eddie usually runs to the closet and hides when we fight. He cries a lot but seems to recover quickly when it's all over.

My friends don't understand why I stay with Eric. They don't understand that we really love each other, that we have this intense thing going—dancing, holding each other close, shutting out the world. That part is heaven, particularly after a fight. Eric can be a very exciting guy. I don't want to lose him.

From a psychological perspective, you might say that Vanessa has very low self-esteem but tries to hold those awful feelings at bay by becoming Eric's heroic, loving rescuer. She's fooling herself, living in a fantasy that could destroy her if allowed to follow its course. As you will see in chapter 3, this self-defeating pattern is very much related to her own past. She has many emotional issues to face.

So what do right and wrong, good and bad, and other moralistic, ethical concerns have to do with Vanessa's situation? Plenty. And how can she be helped if she also begins to view her situation from that perspective? More than she would ever predict.

Lighting the Shadows

In a nutshell, even if Vanessa has little or no awareness of her underlying psychological difficulties, she needs to open her eyes to the moral implications of Eric's behavior as well as her own. Although Eric is ravaged by his own psychological demons, there's more to it than that. He violates some basic principles that most people value. (Chapter 2 will take a closer look at these and other principles or values, where they came from and what they mean.)

- Eric engages in cruel behavior, disregarding principles of *caring*, kindness, and humane treatment.
- He is not *honest* with himself or Vanessa and believes his own excuses.
- He does not act out of *fairness.*
- He shows little if any *respect* for Vanessa's fundamental worth and dignity.
- He sees women as inferior and has little sense of *equality.*
- Eric takes total control and works to undermine Vanessa's basic *liberties* such as freedom of expression and choice.
- He fails in his *responsibility* to his family and their welfare, and places them at great risk.

Although Vanessa is technically the victim here, she needs to recognize her own role in perpetuating this sad situation. Aside from the psychological aspects that keep her clinging to a destructive relationship, Vanessa fails to see some of the larger issues.

- She is less than *honest* with herself, and lies *for* her husband by making up excuses.

- She has gotten caught up in all sorts of psychological "reasons" for Eric's behavior, rather than stating that it is *wrong* and unacceptable.

- She allows herself to be treated *unfairly*, blames herself, and seems to accept Eric's view of women as inferior.

- Vanessa fails to act *responsibly* in protecting her son. She indulges her own needs and hangups (consciously and unconsciously) while her son suffers great harm.

Before anyone accuses me of "blaming the victim," carefully consider each of the observations about Vanessa's role and determine on your own whether they are applicable. These are simply things that are happening for all sorts of complicated reasons. You may use different terms, cite other principles and values, or come up with psychological "causes" (e.g., battered women's syndrome and so forth), but I think you'll agree that the problem is not a cut-and-dried case of victim and victimizer—at least not yet. Both parties, to varying degrees, are contributing to the situation.

The moral consequence of Vanessa's self-destructive cycle may not come into full play until we consider what's happening to her son. He is getting hurt and no one is protecting him. Vanessa may escape our moral gaze if she is hurting only herself, but with her son at risk, she has stepped into the moral arena. True enough, the cold, harsh realities of the world (lack of money, an overburdened judicial system, a shortage of facilities for battered women) may eventually frustrate her efforts to escape or even survive. But at this point, she hasn't asked for any help and fails to see what's really going on.

Powerful Rewards

So what can Vanessa learn if she opens her eyes to the moral aspects of the abusive cycle? For one, she might see that the abuse is just plain wrong, regardless of Eric's difficult childhood. She can learn that she's compromising her own integrity and honesty. She can learn that she doesn't seem to value her own gender. She can learn that she's giving up liberties such as self-determination, choice, and expression. And she can learn that she's neglecting her responsibility as a parent. All of these lessons are powerful and visible without delving into any great psychological insights or possible causes.

But that's not all. As Vanessa begins to identify some of these basic problems, she will work to reclaim the values she has lost. And by doing so, she will begin to feel better about herself, which in turn will thwart the destructive cycle. Furthermore, her potential for having satisfying relationships in the future will be vastly improved. All of these progressions, of course, would be greatly assisted by psychological insight, but the initial steps can be taken with minimal soul-searching. You'll see how Vanessa can actually sort through this in the chapters to come.

Eric, of course, is fending off his own demons. His view of himself, his relationships, and the world has been seriously distorted by a childhood lacking in emotional warmth and consistent parental guidance. His self-deception runs deep, and he has the moral sensitivity of an alligator. In later chapters, you'll see how he got this way and what he can do about it.

> Of course I know it's wrong! Who wouldn't? But she's at me all the time. "Eric, do this, Eric, do that, you're ignoring me, Eric, play with the baby, Eric." I've worked like a dog, gotten myself away from my family, through college, and into a decent job. I don't need her telling me what to do. I got along fine with-

out her. Like most women, give her an inch, she takes a mile. She's got to learn that I'll treat her fairly when she treats me fairly. Deep down, she knows I'm the best thing she's ever had. She's naive about the world and needs my strengths.

Look, if she loves me so much, why does she seem to melt when other guys give her the eye? I can read her like a book, so I blow. I just lose it. Once it starts, I can't stop, like something takes over inside. I hate it. My father had the same problem. I think it's a nerve disorder or something.

THE GREAT BALANCING ACT

David, a forty-seven-year-old corporate attorney, unfulfilled and bored in his job, is having an affair with Shana, age twenty-seven, his vivacious, sexy legal assistant. The dilemma, of course, is that he dearly loves his wife and children, a love that is far deeper than surging impulses and romantic infatuations. He is racked with extraordinary guilt and has fallen into a deep despair, questioning every nuance of his character, his sense of responsibility and commitment, and his resolve in fending off powerful, instinctual forces.

Unforeseen consequences are often triggered when we hurt others. As David later recounts it, a simple slip, a very brief moment in time, changed the course of his life and tore gaping holes in his finely woven web of responsibility.

The journey began with a small but highly charged kiss of gratitude for a birthday present and quickly slid into a deep pit of ecstasy, fluid dreams, and insatiable yearnings for release, over and over again. Feeling trapped but welcoming his magical captor, David relinquished self-control in search of a world without boundaries, where flesh and passion melted the frigid walls of insecurity, separateness, and repressed needs. His guilt triggered a deep depression. As these things often go, the only source of relief appeared to be the fire that ignited his dilemma in the first place. The affair has continued for well over a year.

Sometimes, getting the bigger picture and knowing the right thing to do is not enough. Like Vanessa and Eric, David is caught in a self-destructive cycle. But unlike them, he is more than aware of the moral ramifications of his behavior. He knows that he must choose between conflicting values and newly discovered personal needs—a precarious balancing act that is driving him to despair. In David's case, a healthy dose of psychological insight might help him through the difficult choices, clear his vision, and illuminate the ruts in the road. As you will see throughout this book, self-knowledge and doing the right thing go hand in hand.

I desperately tried to fend off my feelings for Shana, and did so for a long time. But it turned into a highly charged game, like toying with fire, confident that it wouldn't burn out of control. Such exquisite fantasies! It added an addictive spark of excitement and forbidden sensuality to the office grind, the only thing to look forward to. God, but how I suffered! My wife, Noreen, is wonderful, and the kids make my world! The thought of hurting them . . . After Shana and I stepped over the line, I've thought about killing myself many times. But to do that would be to abandon Noreen and the kids. I can't do that.

Why have I done this? It's against everything I believe in. It's not something I would do! I value and aspire to self-control, commitment, responsibility, and honesty. Honesty! But I'm lying to everyone: to Shana, who thinks I'm going to divorce Noreen; to Noreen, who doesn't know about the affair but thinks I'm going through a midlife crisis; to myself. At times I even convince myself that I could run off to an exciting new life with Shana. What a crock! She has a lot of personality problems that I just don't understand. But her raw emotion—her drama—makes me feel so wild, so free, so uninhibited. Am I to give that up? It would be like killing off an exciting new part of myself.

Gaps in the Web of Responsibility

The Lover.   Shana, David's legal assistant and lover, has a long history of hostile entanglements with married men. In each case, she is secretly convinced that her irresistible beauty and passion will prevail. Her powers of seduction will defeat the wife she envies and hates, and will win the perfect object of her fantasies—a man who never leaves her, a man who understands her erratic moods and brings full-ness to her life. Invariably, Mr. Perfect finds himself rele-gated to the pits of hell when he fails to deliver—even if he leaves his wife.

Shana yearns for a relationship to fill her emptiness. But serious personality problems will undermine that quest and obscure her moral vision as well. (We'll take a closer look at her personality problems in chapters 4 and 6.) Quite sur-prisingly, she feels morally justified, even superior, in doing what she does. Shana is the eternal victim, a mass of con-tradictions and distortions.

David is very kind and giving but he is weak. He can't seem to say no to his wife and ends up hurting me in the process. Last Monday he canceled our meeting—something about his kid being sick—and left me alone for the evening. The wife can take care of the kid, but what about me? I felt so hurt, angry, and alone, I grabbed a paring knife and scratched a teardrop in the thigh he loves to caress. He'll be see-ing it for a long time to come, to remind him how un-fair and hurtful he can be. He understands nothing about women.

He's ridden with guilt and he should be. Look what he's doing to me, to his family! I don't think I could ever trust him again. Plus, I've heard him lie to *her* over the phone. What kind of crap is he telling me? Yes, I lie to him, but he leaves me little choice in the matter.

He says he loves me. If he loved me, he'd be here, *now*. I don't think he knows what love is other than the throbbing in his pants. Yes, I've cheated on him, but that's what he gets. He can't go around taking advantage, abusing people like this. And this man is my boss. Think of it! A lawyer who's blind to sexual harassment? Whether he knows it or not, he has power over my career as well as my emotional life. There is absolutely nothing fair about this situation.

The Spouse.   Noreen, David's wife of twenty years and a public relations consultant, has been reading one self-help book after another, looking for anything that might explain her husband's dismal moods and preoccupations. Although there have been many clues that David is indeed having an affair, Noreen hasn't allowed herself to see them. She is convinced that David is going through a "midlife crisis"—as if the broad term itself provides an adequate explanation.

She knows David as a good, virtuous person and simply can't imagine that he would jeopardize their marriage for an immature sexual romp. In Noreen's way of thinking, a strong, loving relationship with good sex is the foremost safeguard against infidelity. While this may be true to a great extent, it is incomplete and underestimates the powerful forces that work to undermine our best intentions. There is only so much that Noreen can do. The rest depends upon, among other things, David's values, his strength in carrying out his moral ideals, and his level of self-awareness.

I just don't know what's wrong with David. He sits and stares all the time, like something is sapping his energy. When I ask about it, he insists that nothing's wrong other than his job. He's still kind and considerate but it's as if he's not with us anymore. Even the kids are upset about it. I keep asking him if it's me or something, our relationship. I've even suggested marriage counseling, which, of course, he rejects. "There's nothing wrong with us," he says. "I'm just tired and need some space."

We still make love, but it's like going through the motions, like he's holding back for some reason. It was never like that before. Should I follow him around to see if there's someone else? That would be an incredible breach of trust. I don't believe he would ever do such a thing. Besides, I know that he loves me and wouldn't intentionally do anything to hurt me.

I know most men go through this sort of thing at his age—feeling that they've missed out, wanting something more but not knowing what, coming to grips with their limitations. I'm surprised, though, because David has never been like most men. He's never been one to go out with the guys, fool around, or follow some pipe dream. His family has always come first. Maybe he's clinically depressed. Maybe he needs something like Prozac. I'm starting to get scared and don't know what to do. I find myself crying all the time.

The Oldest Son. Richard, age nineteen, David and Noreen's oldest son, has also been snared in the traps laid by his father's affair. A first-year computer engineering student at a prestigious technical institute, Richard is having great difficulty in an electrical engineering course and is considering cheating on a major exam. If caught, he would face expulsion or at the very least a suspension and the loss of his partial scholarship. Richard's attendance at the school has been the fulfillment of a family dream. A large chunk of income is earmarked for Richard's tuition.

It's stupid, I know, but it's like I don't have much of a choice. I'm nearly failing, anyhow. Some guy has gotten hold of an exam and is selling it. All sorts of people are springing for it, so a group of us might buy one and share the information. It's like if I don't, I'll be screwed, at the bottom of the heap. The competition is ferocious and the course is a bear. It's like the prof doesn't give a damn about our other course loads, like his is the only one in the world. The guy's an egotistical jerk. I know it's wrong to cheat, but it doesn't even seem like cheating because everyone is doing it.

Either way, my dad would kill me—fail the course or pass by cheating. And if I get caught and expelled, it might even kill him. For the past year he's been like a robot. He doesn't do a damned thing except get on my case. He says that I spend too much time with my girlfriend, that I'm ignoring my studies, that I'm going to blow the whole thing. I'm really sick of his harassment. All he thinks about anymore is money, winning, losing, and work. Well, I'm not the robot he is. I love him but he's an incredible bore. The guy needs to loosen up. Sometimes you just have to say "screw it."

THE HEART OF THE MATTER

Like Vanessa and Eric, the couple in the physically abusive relationship, David, Shana, Noreen, and Richard are all struggling with a delicate balance, or imbalance, involving several important personal qualities or skills. These skills lie at the core of doing the right thing, and are reflected in the following questions:

- *How will my actions affect other people? How much? What's at stake?* This is the ability to see that certain situations have moral implications, that others might be harmed or helped.

- *Will I be violating my standards and any larger values?* This is the knowledge of moral values, like those cited for Vanessa and Eric.

- *Am I misjudging the situation because of my own needs or interests? Can I control myself while I think this through?* These questions pertain to self-knowledge and self-control.

- *Are some choices morally better than others? Why?* This requires the ability to reason through moral choices.

- *Do I have the willpower and courage to do what I think is right?* This is the strength to carry out what one thinks should be done.

You'll learn more about these important skills in future chapters and how they apply to the characters in our moral theater. We'll find out where these skills come from, the best way to develop them, and how they often get left behind when we are faced with a moral dilemma. All sorts of fascinating dramas come into play when our moral and psychological sensitivities are roused by such problems. Some might even say that these dramas lie at the heart of our emotional and spiritual development.

THOSE NAGGING LITTLE QUESTIONS

Before going any further on this journey, we need to consider some important questions that have undoubtedly crossed your mind. I've done my best to avoid them but the time has come. These questions reflect some messy little philosophical concerns that are guaranteed to bring on massive headaches. And, quite frankly, they turn many people off. The answers seem to change with the eye of the beholder. A sampling:

- "This right and wrong business is annoying. Right for whom? Things are never so simple."

- "Why should I care about putting things in a moral perspective? I try not to hurt other people. Isn't that good enough?"

- "What's all this 'goodness' rhetoric, anyway? I don't even know what it means. You haven't defined the term or any other terms for that matter."

- "After all, isn't 'goodness' a relative term like a 'good' Nazi, a 'good' terrorist, a 'good' Catholic or Jew? Who's setting the standards?"

- "What if being a 'good' person is irrelevant in this world? Maybe it's a simplistic fantasy that's made up by those in power to keep the masses in control."

- "What if I don't believe in some supreme entity or heaven? Who am I trying to impress? Am I supposed to be good—whatever that means—to avoid punishment?"

- "No one likes a moralistic, judgmental, self-righteous bigot. How can a person pay attention to moral concerns without falling into this trap?"

It would be easy to drown in all sorts of philosophical arguments here. And I'm sure that your questions go far beyond these. But the practical information we need is really at our fingertips and requires very little philosophical hemming and hawing. Certainly, we can't figure everything out, but we can glean enough to make our lives more manageable and rewarding. To answer some of these questions without drowning, we need to take a slight detour and find out what this morality business is all about—the subject of the next chapter. No sermons. I promise.

TWO

The Dreaded "M" Word: "Pipe Down, Preacher"

Morality. Before you throw the book down in anticipation of platitudes and a nasty list of dos and don'ts, goods and bads, let me assure you that I might have the same gut reaction.

Indeed, if recent surveys are accurate, the word "morality" is a powder keg for many of us, evoking images of self-righteous crusades, intolerance, and expedient justifications for whatever biases we hold. Since morality involves the drawing of lines, it can be a very dangerous concept—particularly in times like these when so many forces are calling for "a return to morality." Suddenly, every politician is blathering about morality. It's getting to be a bit much.

But what are we really talking about here? Considering the slippery state of the world and the inevitable rise of people who know "the way," it behooves us all to reconsider the meaning of morality. If we don't, someone else will do it for us.

TO PURGATORY AND BACK

It's really not so difficult to get a handle on what morality is all about. To begin, let me illustrate with a small personal experience that profoundly changed the way I view the world. Although I remain the logical "scientific" psychologist, the experience has sparked a new dimension of understanding of the human condition and how we relate to each other.

During the summer of 1992 I found myself in the hospital, tubes hanging out of every orifice, a five-inch gash on my right side where they had removed a badly infected, burst appendix. My body obviously had been trying to tell me something for days, but I had stubbornly ignored the pain, assuming that it was stress-related. The vague stomachache crept into my life the morning a friend succumbed to cancer, disappeared entirely the day of his funeral, then returned with a vengeance. So this was the price to pay for self-diagnosis. The nurses smiled knowingly as they stuck yet another needle into my veins, with daily reassurances, "You'd probably be dead by now if it weren't for these new antibiotics."

The worst of it was not the pain or the ten-day confinement but the nightly "dreams" that persisted, even when I was half awake. I felt reasonably certain that they were drug-induced; nevertheless, the nocturnal excursions were so real, so terrifying that they shook me to the core. Knowing the probable source did not in any way diminish the impact of the experience. I can still feel the cold sweats.

Every time I closed my eyes, I found myself falling into an absolutely horrific, mechanistic world governed by strict cause and effect, with no inkling whatsoever of human feelings or caring. Human life in this dark vision existed on some basic level but the individuals were not emotionally connected in any way. Their humanity was as empty and brutal as a train plowing through a car or a bulldozer pushing bodies at Auschwitz.

Since drives and goals were primary for these imaginary people in my visions, nothing stood in their way. They followed certain strict rules of relating, just as a computer predictably follows a program, but consideration and caring were intellectual terms that held no specific meanings. It was a cold, vacuous, terrifying world. Quite simply, there appeared to be no love, empathy, or emotional core for relating to each other—and it was absolute hell, evil.

To make matters worse, during these dreams I experienced a sense of complete physical and psychological disintegration. Elements of my personality were reduced to digital bits drifting around like flotsam in a dark sea. Without the love, the interconnectedness, there was little if anything, holding me together. It became obvious that this missing cohesion was the most important quality in the world, the universe—something that I had intuitively known but taken for granted. Until now, I hadn't truly comprehended the depth of it. Without this unifying force, this harmony, I was nothing.

Each morning I awoke to the joyous sounds of the nurses laughing and bickering. Even in moments of discontent and anger, their eyes held the core of my own existence. Nothing would be quite the same again.

Several days after discharge I was able to walk out to the Charles River near our home in Boston. It was a magnificent day. As I gazed across the water, a strange, almost orgiastic feeling set in. The world sparkled with a glowing vibrancy that I had never seen before. Each leaf, tree, blade of grass, grain of dirt—everything—danced in a brilliant, radiant harmony; a stream of notes in a universal symphony. The intensity swelled to a crescendo and I was released, a wave dissolving in a golden sea. Here was the force, the power and soul that was absent in my mechanistic dreams. And I had been surrounded by it all the time, sensing but unseeing.

This heightened sensitivity to our sea of beauty persisted, to a lesser extent, for several days. I was unable to read an engrossing novel and listen to music at the same time. Each activity was in itself overwhelmingly alive, vibrant, and consuming. The ethereal beauty of an aria in Brahms' Alto Rhapsody, the light playing on our golden barrel cactus, the ladybug on my arm—each held a special, deeply felt mystery, the essence of all that was good. I was later to learn that my friend, who knew he was dying of cancer, had similar experiences of heightened awareness. As the rational psychologist who normally valued evidence over belief, he hesitated to tell other people.

Since I am not one for hasty conclusions, I also was extremely hesitant and even embarrassed to tell anyone. But in another sense, I felt a pressing obligation to do so. Unfortunately, the words used to convey such feelings are inadequate and come off as trite clichés. We've heard them all before. But this does not in any way diminish the power of the experience.

What was at the root of it? A neurochemical reaction to the body trauma? A spiritual awakening? Or was I indeed deluded and hysterical? Take your pick. It really doesn't matter, at least to me. My journey into the dark revealed the full force of the light in which we live. It allowed me to see and *feel* the sheer horror of a strictly functional world without soul, without love, caring, relation, and passion. I could experience myself, such as I was, as an empty, meaningless vessel with no connection whatsoever to a larger whole. The unifying light, the force that permeates and enlivens every particle of our world, was gone. So was my spirit and soul.

Perhaps evil is indeed a way of illuminating the good that we take for granted. My re-entry into our imperfect, troubled world was a rush of nirvana and beauty. In spite of the presence of destructive forces, here was the profoundly remarkable core of life, our whole, flowing within and around us, touching sinners and saints alike. Here was the quality missing from my nightmare vision.

Although the kernels of caring and humanity are often obscured by the dark in our world, they lie within each of us, awaiting the light. With few exceptions, even the most vicious killers among us care about and feel with someone else. This is our spiritual connection, our link with all that is miraculous. The thread of goodness, of love, is pervasive and undeniable. We are nothing without it.

The Essence of Morality

So what does this have to do with morality? Quite simply, *morality is derived from love, the core of our existence, the all-encompassing thread of goodness that allows us to feel for and with others.* Morality is the inevitable, necessary consequence of our immense capacity for caring and concern. It is the standard by which we relate to one another, the product and protector of our loving essence. Like the air we breathe, like love, our moral universe surrounds us, whether we are aware of it or not. It's central to our welfare and lies at the core of our meaningful existence as human beings. And, like air and love, morality all too often becomes evident only when polluted or absent. We all need to be more receptive to the power and beauty of our moral universe.

But you don't need to buy my interpretation as any kind of "truth." Just think about it. The very fact that most of us have the *capacity* and *need* to feel for other human beings and other forms of life, to feel their pain, to consider their needs, to treat them with fairness, and to refrain from hurting them, is ample evidence for the existence of our moral quality. Without it, humankind would self-destruct in a mechanistic shambles.

Most certainly, there is evil in the world. But for every individual or group of individuals lost in the dark realm of hurting others, there are tens of millions of good people who would risk their lives to help and protect their fellows. Furthermore, this core of goodness can be extended to our relationship with all that we value: animals, the environment, the enhancement and preservation of art and beauty, the special things and objects that hold meaning, spirit, and life. This is the predominant way of our universe and should be kept in mind when the world dips in and out of bleakness. Even under the most dire conditions, the sense of humanity, of goodness, can be obscured but never destroyed. Ask those who survived the gas chambers of Auschwitz or the jungles of Vietnam.

For the most part, people in our moral universe are good because they want to be good. As you will see in chapter 3, the threat of punishment plays only a very small role in the majority of our moral experiences. Most of us, excluding our resident psychopaths and hard-core criminals, consider the needs of other people because we want to. It makes us feel good. *Our personal sense of goodness, then, depends a great deal upon our capacity to feel and behave in a concerned, caring manner.* We'll look at this more closely in the chapters to come.

BREATHING HUMANITY INTO HELL

To understand what the moral universe is all about, we need to identify some of the basic building blocks that underlie our daily existence as well as our relationships. At this point, we're simply looking for the basic principles or values that allow us to coexist with other human beings, other life forms, and our environment. We can find these principles by using our capacity for *reasoning*, regardless of any religious beliefs we may hold. For the moment, set aside any qualms you may have about semantics, interpretations, practical applications, or religious concerns.

Imagine yourself an observer in the mechanistic universe similar to the one in my nightmares. The inhabitants have flesh and blood and look like human beings, but they behave like machines or computers. Power rules. Their intellectual efforts center on the assessment of power potentials, logistics, and tactics to get what they need for survival in a world of limited resources. Nothing deters them except a stronger force. They live in an eternal cold war.

If you had the power to do so, what important qualities would you add to improve their lives and increase their chances for survival? Looking for various perspectives on the matter, I informally posed the dilemma to a number of people around Boston. Here's a sample of their responses:

High school teacher: "They need to be able to feel each other's pain, to relate to the harm they are inflicting, to put themselves in the other guy's shoes. Then they must learn to share what they have, figure out some way to distribute resources fairly, and cooperate with each other. Even animals cooperate to some extent."

Waiter in an East Indian restaurant: "Love, love, love, as well as the realization that they are part of a larger consciousness. They need a sense of responsibility toward the whole, to the universe and their society, above and beyond a responsibility toward their own needs."

First-year law student: "Well, obviously they need to be able to care about each other, call it love, whatever. But that's not enough. They need to agree on some rules, rules of conduct and punishment, rules for earning and using resources, and rules about property rights. Guess I'm sounding like a lawyer, but these things are important."

Cab driver: "You name it—all the good stuff—love, respect, kindness, consideration, compassion, responsibility, honesty, fairness. What else can I say? I think I drove through your nightmare last night."

Police officer: "Jesus! Sounds like the gang wars around here. Sounds like my job. We're all going down the tubes fast, like those poor saps. We—they—need respect, respect for themselves and others, for the law, as well as a sense of commitment and duty. Nobody gives a damn anymore. They're just out for their friggin' selves. Whatever happened to right and wrong? Everybody's got excuses these days, nobody's responsible. And our courts are a joke! It's all heading toward your hell . . . and I think I'm already in it! Thank God for my family."

Substance abuse counselor: "Oh, God! Where to start! Feelings and respect for others have to come first, otherwise it would be impossible. Then they need to learn to share, to be fair. They must stop doing things to hurt each other. And they must balance off personal needs with those of the common good, otherwise they're doomed as a society. They also need to be able to control their primitive impulses and take responsibility for their actions."

Librarian: "You're talking about all the elements of the moral universe here, all that's good, all that holds people and societies together. They need moral values, values that philosophers, theologians, and other great thinkers have found to be tried and true throughout the centuries. They work. Plus they give meaning to life. What are they? Well, dignity of life, truth, loyalty, responsibility, justice, respect, humaneness, freedom, helpfulness ... these things have stood the test of time. I'd also give them religion and faith. It's tough to go it alone, without a higher purpose."

Seven-year-old child from Ethiopia: "They need to learn it's bad to hurt each other." How do you know it's bad? "Everybody knows that, don't you know that? If I hurt someone they might hurt me back or stop being my friend." How do you feel when you see someone being hurt? "Bad. Sometimes I cry when they cry."

Chances are you came up with a similar list of qualities, regardless of your religious or philosophical background or your ethnicity. Most of these qualities can be deduced by a simple reasoning process. They make sense and feel right.

THE INCREDIBLE SEVEN

In studies all over the world, psychologists and other researchers have identified a range of overlapping values that seem to make up the moral universe. These are values that have repeatedly withstood the test of time and are considered by most people to be important for human survival and the quality of life. With a few exceptions, their general acceptance is remarkably consistent across cultures. Individuals, of course, usually interpret, weigh, and apply these values differently. That's the difficult part.

In essence, most people aspire to be treated in the manner prescribed by these values—even if their cultures or governments fail to respect these aspirations. This, incidentally, is a good test of any moral value—ask yourself, "Would I want it applied to me or my loved ones?"

Here are seven essential values that appear to lie at the foundation of our moral universe. You may remember some of them from chapter 1, where they were used to size up

Eric's abusive relationship with Vanessa. Although there are seven separate values listed here, they tend to overlap in many respects. Sometimes it's difficult to know where one value ends and another begins. Semantics and hazy definitions aside, these values can serve as very useful guidelines for our moral behavior. Many other values have been derived from these basic seven.

BENCHMARK NO. 1
THE INCREDIBLE SEVEN:
KEY VALUES IN OUR MORAL UNIVERSE

1. **Justice and Fairness:** Equal, unbiased treatment, sharing, tolerance of differences.

2. **Caring:** Kindness, compassion, humane treatment, cooperation, following the Golden Rule: "Do unto others as you would have them do unto you."

3. **Respect:** Regard for the fundamental worth and dignity of every human being, including oneself. Intending no harm, if at all possible. Respect for the rights and properties of others. Respect for other life forms and the environment.

4. **Responsibility:** Responding to the needs of others, looking out for their welfare, making commitments, carrying out duties for the "larger good," fulfilling obligations. Self-discipline.

5. **Honesty:** Dealing honestly with people, maintaining integrity.

6. **Loyalty:** Keeping promises, maintaining trust and fidelity, respecting confidences, honoring just laws and policies.

7. **Liberty:** The right to self-determination, freedom of choice and expression, freedom from slavery, and so forth. (This value seems to vary more than the others from culture to culture.)

DIFFERENT STROKES
FOR DIFFERENT FOLKS?

Some values, of course, are not universal. The other day, while riding the subway, I sat across from a young woman with bright vermilion hair, a pierced nostril, and a tiny butterfly tattoo on her right shoulder. Her friend, standing in the aisle, appeared understated and "sensible" in a simple peasant dress. They were engaged in a heated discussion about an upcoming meeting of some sort concerning feminist ideals and policy.

"Sandra, you've got to come. You can't cop out like this!" implored the friend in the aisle. "Don't you believe in equality and empowerment? And don't you think we have a moral obligation to fight for the things we believe in?"

Sandra, growing increasingly agitated at the moral inveigling, snapped, "Yes, Judy, yes! But I'm sick and tired of the woman-as-victim routine, the rhetoric, and the siege mentality. And I've had it with this academic, liberal, elitist stuff. It's not what most women are about."

Taken aback, Judy glared at her friend and spoke deliberately. "I really don't know what's happened to your values, Sandra. I think you're headed in a dangerous direction."

Sandra rose from her seat and headed for the door. "My values are evolving. They're not stuck in some 1980s rut like yours. Wake up! And tell your friends to wake up." She disappeared out the door.

Not All Values Are Moral Values

Some values are simply personal preferences (jazz, pierced nostrils, Thai food, quiet friends) and don't have much to do with morality. Sandra's appearance falls into this neutral realm, although some might argue otherwise. On the other hand, the values voiced by Judy represent moral obligations—things that she feels she should do—based on her political beliefs as well as on her interpretations of the larger universal values cited above. Sandra seems to hold similar moral values about equality and respect but she has different ideas about how those ends might be achieved. In each woman, we see a mix of moral and nonmoral values.

Group Values Are Not Always Universal

Obviously, many of the values that people feel obligated to follow are based on their particular religious or political beliefs and vary greatly across cultures. They are not necessarily universal, although the individuals espousing these values will often say they are "for the larger good." Meditating six times daily and renouncing material possessions reflect one nonuniversal value system, while acquiring wealth and using it to help others reflect another.

Condemning a person's sexual preference, disapproving of sexual practices that harm no one, and requiring women to wear veils are also nonuniversal values. These values are often related to specific individuals, religions, or societies and need to be weighed against the standards set by the universal moral values. This can be a very difficult task.

Sometimes nonuniversal values and the means used to achieve them are clearly destructive, as in the case of white supremacy, the rhetoric of hate found in neo-Nazism, or the terrorist activity of certain religious zealots and political extremists. Perhaps the groups holding these values justify their actions as "moral duties" to God or country, but they overlook the equality of human rights and fail to respect the dignity of people as individuals. Their morality is tied to political or obscure religious norms. It violates universal moral values and misses the larger picture. We need only remember the painful images of the Oklahoma City terrorist bombing to understand the consequences of an inhumane moral vision.

LIFE'S LITTLE COMPLICATIONS

The universal moral values can serve as principled guidelines for any moral decisions that we make. But there are a few catches that lie at the core of our development as moral human beings. First, our understanding, interpretation, and application of the universal moral values in any particular situation may be totally at odds with someone else's perception of the problem. And second, more often than not, we must make difficult choices between any number of good alternatives, worthy claims, and justifiable reasons. Even worse, sometimes there are no good choices. This is the stuff of life, the boot camp that builds character and enlightens souls. Right and wrong are not always clear or absolute.

For example, what would you do in the following situations?

• You saw your husband's boss leaving a motel room with your brother's wife. Telling your brother may jeopardize your husband's job and the security of your family. What is the fair thing to do? And what does *fair* mean in this situation anyway? Fair to whom? Your sister-in-law probably has different ideas about it, even if she acknowledges wrongdoing. What about loyalty? Is loyalty to your brother more important than the responsibility you have for maintaining the stability of your own family? Although you deeply care about everyone involved, whose well-being must prevail here? How about honesty? Must the truth be told at any expense? Perhaps you should forget and deny the whole thing, even if your brother fishes for clues as his suspicions grow.

• Your close friend and roommate, Jerry, has been diagnosed HIV-positive. He swears you to secrecy and tells you that the condom broke last night while he was sleeping with Paula, the local sexual butterfly. The problem is, he refuses to tell Paula, stating "You know the rumors. She's probably got it already. Besides, she'll tell everybody and my goose'll be cooked. What am I supposed to do, avoid sex for the rest of my life? I tried to be safe but it was an accident. She got too wild."

Since you can gain access to the computer data banks at the only medical laboratory in the area, you consider looking up Paula's record. That would be a serious violation of your employment contract. But if she is already infected, you and Jerry might be off the hook. Maybe.

What's more important—respecting Paula's right to privacy or your responsibility to other people who might become infected? If she is infected, do you have a right to tell others who you know have slept with her? What about telling Brian and Tim, two other friends who have expressed an interest in her? Either way, is it fair to Paula if you sit back and say nothing to her about Jerry's HIV status? Do you still owe Jerry loyalty, even though he is dealing deceptively with people? What is your responsibility for the larger good?

• You are the CEO of a financially strapped fertilizer company employing three hundred workers in a small Midwestern town. In order to survive, you must merge with a larger corporation. You and your board are secretly considering offers from two major conglomerates. In one, your job would be redefined as a middle management position and two hundred workers would be let go. In the other, you would be given a top management position in the parent company and all employees would be retained. However, under these terms, your company would be retooled to produce highly toxic pesticides.

How do you balance your responsibility to yourself and your family, your employees, and the community at large? How can you look out for the rights and well-being of some while hurting others? Is that fair and just? In whose eyes? Would you want your own family to live and work in a potentially toxic environment? And by keeping the negotiations secret, aren't you denying others the right of self-determination? But if you were more open, might the ensuing protests undermine the negotiations, sinking the company and destroying the town's major employer?

You may be able to solve these dilemmas quickly and to your own satisfaction without much angst: Keep your mouth shut, tell your brother nothing about his wayward wife; tell your roommate Jerry that if he doesn't get over there and tell Paula he is HIV-positive, you'll tell her yourself; go with the merger for the top management position, retain the employees, and, using your new power, figure out later how to reduce the toxic hazard. Easy, right? Sometimes, but not always. Other people in your life might see things differently.

Decisions, Decisions

Deciding what to do can, at times, be an extremely painful process as we weigh what we ought to do, what our conscience and feelings tell us to do, and which values are most important to us. Compromises are inevitable as we attempt to balance competing interests and determine which values are paramount in a particular situation. We rarely have all of the universal moral values on our side. We are always having to choose between good answers, although some answers may be better than others. Nevertheless, the questions are everywhere:

- Should I follow a law if I think it's unjust?
- Is it worth it to blow the whistle at work, or should I just look the other way?
- How far should I go in promoting my own interests? When other people are affected, where's the line?
- Should I stand behind my political party if its policies violate my personal standards?
- How much would I lie to protect family and friends?
- Would I be willing to hurt some people, like firing them at work, if I knew many more would ultimately benefit by my cost-cutting action? Or would it be better to do nothing?

Although the choices often seem overwhelming as we set our course, the universal moral values can illuminate what's at stake, what our compromises might entail, and whether we have strayed from humane ideals. In chapter 9, you'll find a case example illustrating how these values can help you sort through tough moral dilemmas. In the meantime, we need to add another essential piece to the moral universe.

THE GREAT LINK BETWEEN MORALITY AND PSYCHOLOGY

Remember David, the married attorney having an affair with Shana, his legal assistant? (See page 12 for the beginning of their story.) David is on the brink of killing himself in spite of the immense pleasure he is experiencing with Shana.

> It's eating me up inside. I'm so ashamed and disgusted with myself. But those feelings still don't give me the strength to get out of the relationship. It's almost as if I've accepted and gotten used to feelings of shame. This is who I am, so why fight it? That may not be true but that's what it feels like. Sometimes I can almost see the disapproval in other people's eyes, even when I'm certain they know nothing about the affair. What hurts the most, however, the thing that's killing me, is the knowledge that I'm hurting my wife, Noreen, and my family. The guilt drills into the pit of my stomach and never leaves.

The Voice of Conscience

Although David is not a religious person, he carries within him a set of personal standards that have triggered much of his pain. The pain, although excruciating, is a valuable, persistent beacon that something is wrong. His affair is violating his concepts of right and wrong, his values concerning the treatment of other people, and his image of himself. David is violating that inner voice we all know as *con-*

science. Now we are approaching the realm of personal psychology, as well as morality.

Our conscience tells us that there is a "right" thing to do, even if we are not certain what it is, makes us feel *obligated* to do it, and admonishes us to *control* our destructive impulses and temptations. While the right thing to do may be different for different individuals, people with a fully developed conscience will experience varying degrees of *guilt* if they fail to treat others according to these inner standards. Like David, they may also experience disgust with themselves or *shame.* Chances are, right now, you can think of something you have done in the past that triggers an immediate, visceral pang in your body. This is the enduring power of conscience.

Learning from Shame and Guilt

Shame and guilt are related but they are not the same thing. David feels badly about himself, the person he has become. This is the essence of shame—an overall sense of inadequacy and failure as a person. His guilt, on the other hand, is specifically related to the bad deed he is committing against his wife and other people. He feels guilty because he is hurting them. *Guilt arises out of concern for others; shame arises from a sense of personal failure.*

If, by some miracle of strength, David can get out of this mess, he may be able to allay much but not necessarily all of his guilt. By making sincere amends and asking for and receiving true forgiveness, he will be taking major steps in that direction. His shame, however, may be more difficult to handle.

Shackled by Shame

Since shame is really a feeling about one's self, it can be tough to overcome. Often, it is self-perpetuating. We can see the beginning of this problem in David's statement, "It's almost as if I've accepted and gotten used to feelings of shame.

This is who I am, so why fight it?" How he feels about himself will influence future actions, which, in turn, might reinforce his negative view of himself. Although shame is a natural, often helpful reaction when we violate values, it also has the potential to immobilize rather than motivate.

In chapter 1, we looked at the story of Eric and Vanessa. (Their story begins on page 7). Eric, you may remember, is the twenty-six-year-old assistant retail manager who emotionally browbeats and physically abuses Vanessa, his wife. Eric, like David, is also fending off enormous feelings of shame. But unlike David, most of Eric's shame is beyond his immediate awareness. Even worse, he barely experiences any guilt at all. It's almost as if he's blinded by shame and anger. His guilt is essentially blocked, resulting in little motivation to change.

> As I said, I don't know why I lose it like I do. Must have a hair trigger like my dad. I couldn't do anything right for that guy—look at him cross-eyed and he'd pound me into the ground like I was nothing. I couldn't fight back, so I just took it. Yeah, I felt bad about myself for years, a real wimp. I'll never let that happen again. I've gotten stronger, to feel better about myself.
>
> I feel guilty when I first see Vanessa cry, but then I get mad because I know she's just trying to jerk me around. She'll cry to avoid blame. But at least she's learning to hit back. Sometimes we all have to hurt to change. That's how I learned.

Eric's sense of shame, personal weakness, and humiliation have been haunting him for years. Although he was not responsible for the childhood abuse, he still harbors feelings of failure and is confused about issues of blame and responsibility: "Perhaps if I had been a stronger person—the son my father always wanted—he would have respected me more." Eric has great difficulty holding his father accountable. He may detest his father but he still aspires to be as powerful as his father appeared to be.

Eric's shame is directly related to his immoral behavior. The sheer force of it has seriously compromised his ability to think clearly and behave morally toward those he loves. He has lived with the hurt for so long that much of it is beyond his immediate awareness. Nevertheless, it erupts periodically as a raging storm against Vanessa. His mind game is to blame Vanessa for his inadequacies. He will control her even if he can't control himself. A major key for change, at least for Eric, is to fully acknowledge the depth of shame and weakness that he experiences. This, in turn, can reawaken his capacity for guilt—an essential ingredient in our moral universe.

Good Guilt, Bad Guilt

Guilt grows out of *empathy,* our amazing ability to feel for others, to put ourselves in their shoes, and to experience indirectly their pain or joy—even the feelings of people we don't know. If we harm someone for whom we feel empathy, most of us experience guilt. Guilt is painful, just like the hurt we may inflict upon others. So, in most cases, it's an invaluable warning sign that something is wrong, that we are being unfair or neglecting our responsibilities. Morally speaking, most guilt is good.

- Good guilt serves as a compass for your personal standards.
- Good guilt helps you to control destructive, hurtful impulses.
- Good guilt makes it possible for you to live more fully and honestly with other human beings.
- Good guilt allows you to experience the pain of your mistakes and take corrective actions.
- Good guilt, if honestly acknowledged, can lead to personal growth, the making of amends, and perhaps even forgiveness.

But guilt is not always good. Sheila feels guilty because she flattened a darting chipmunk on the road. Mary feels shame for eating too much and guilty for disappointing her critical husband. Claudia feels guilty whenever she visits her ailing mother in the nursing home. Robert feels guilty because his daughter was molested by a trusted neighbor. Robert's daughter feels guilty because she imagines she did something to encourage the neighbor. Susan feels guilty because she has married against the wishes of her cloying parents. Carl is ashamed of his sexual fantasies and guilty because he avoids his slovenly wife. Vanessa feels guilty because she sneaks out to see the friends Eric dislikes.

It's easy to drive yourself silly with unnecessary, self-punishing guilt like this. The trick is to be able to tell the good guilt from the bad guilt. Bad guilt, as in the examples, has few moral implications even though it may feel excruciating. You are not really acting immorally or responsible for harming anyone—but it feels as if you are. The guilt is undeserved, unfair, inhibiting, and unproductive.

- Guilt is not helpful when it stems from things that are truly not your fault.
- Guilt is not helpful when you have unintentionally hurt or neglected someone, although apologies may be in order.
- Guilt is not helpful when it's unfairly used by others to manipulate you or impede your personal growth.
- Guilt is not helpful when the hurtful acts were not foreseeable or preventable.
- Guilt is not helpful when your thoughts, feelings, or actions didn't actually hurt anyone else.

Sorting through good guilt and bad guilt is not always an easy matter. It takes a lot of soul-searching to honestly size up the limits of your personal responsibility. But if you don't do this, you run the risk of devoting too much of your emotional energy to things that can't be changed. Even worse, you may avoid or repress good guilt. Repressed guilt (and shame) of any kind can sap your spirit, bring on depression, and keep you mired in the past. But when good guilt is repressed, you are depriving yourself of an extremely valuable resource.

SO WHY IS THE WORLD SUCH A MESS?

Good question. We've got all kinds of moral building blocks and we're surrounded by billions of individuals who consider themselves good people. (Aren't *you*, in fact, basically a good person?) So what's the problem?

Doing the right thing and treating others with kindness and fairness may be an admirable goal, but life is never so simple. Aside from the difficulty of interpreting, weighing, and applying the seven universal moral values, if we even bother to do that at all, we are faced with our own psychological limitations. Try as we might to be rational and objective, our emotional bugaboos and personal biases can sabotage the best of intentions and provide fuel for the worst. (See chapters 5 and 6 for some of the startling mind games we play with ourselves and others.)

But that's not all of it. As you know only too well, some people have a stronger moral sense than others—the woman down the street who's a second mother and confidante to everyone, as opposed to the gossip around the corner who spreads malicious rumors. Why do some people seem to lack a moral capacity? What goes wrong? And where does our capacity for empathy, caring, and kindness come from? What's the best way to nurture it? In the next chapter, we'll add a few more fascinating characters to our moral theater and search the crucible of childhood for clues to our moral sense.

THREE

Where Our Moral Sense Starts: "Such a Good Kid"

Zachary slips out of his Armani jacket and carefully positions himself in the arms of a leather wing chair. He is only twenty-three years old, but his manner is sophisticated, poised, and charming. His countenance is sharp, with piercing blue eyes and a perfect array of sparkling teeth. His golden locks are swept back into a small ponytail. Sipping on a gin and tonic, he leans down to lightly caress Lori's soft neck as she curls up on the red Bokhara rug. He inhales the sweet scent on his fingertips and whispers something about a delicious, succulent plum, to be plucked and savored.

To Zachary, life has indeed been a plum. Wealthy parents, prep school, an Ivy League college, stunning good looks, intelligence, an endless supply of adoring women. What more could he ask for? A gullible jury, for one thing. Zachary is facing his second charge of mail fraud.

It seems that Zachary devised a clever scheme that bilked thousands of Midwestern senior citizens by exploiting their patriotic and religious sentiments. He formed a phony foundation that claimed to support a number of no-nonsense political candidates. His telemarketing and letter campaign conveyed a powerful sense of urgency and moralistic fervor that quickly shifted to harassment if the contributions stopped. Little did his victims know that they were subsidizing Zachary's good life.

Zachary was a good kid, or so it seemed. He was an exceptional student and won several commendations for initiating and carrying out social programs through his church. His

40

family was highly regarded in the community. His parents, in fact, were known as strong disciplinarians who kept their youngsters under extremely tight rein. Their ethic was one of strict rules, obedience, sound moral values, and hard work.

Zachary's only adolescent scrape with the law occurred when he was seventeen. He had ordered thousands of dollars of computer equipment using a credit card he claimed to have found. His father quickly paid the bill and the charges were dropped. Zachary pleaded for his father's forgiveness, crying that it was a stupid prank, a little game with his friends that had gotten out of hand. Glib as always, he said that he had intended to cancel the order the next day but became preoccupied with homework.

Four years later, Zachary was arrested on his first mail fraud charge and placed on probation. His parents severed relations at that time. Quite surprisingly, Zachary continues to donate time and money to local charities. He insists that he has a moral obligation to do so. The tributes he has received from the charities are testaments to his good character. Or so he thinks.

Mrs. Egan sits across from the therapist, eyes brimming with tears behind her silver bifocals. Jennifer, her fifteen-year-old granddaughter, hides behind a flurry of amber hair and stares impassively at the floor. The natural flow of her lithe figure is broken by a protruding abdomen, indicating the second trimester of pregnancy. Like Nanna, her grandmother, Jennifer is dressed in white and smells faintly of croissants and cinnamon rolls. Nanna apologizes and explains that they have just come from her gourmet pastry shop on Cape Cod. She begins their story:

> Jenny has always been so sweet, so bright, I can hardly believe this is happening. First the pregnancy and now this! As you can see, she doesn't want to be here but it's a condition of her probation. For the love of God, I can't understand how she could have done

this to another human being. Does she look like someone who would carry a knife and actually use it? She
says the girl hit her first, but to retaliate with a knife?
It's like she's a different person, from a different kind
of family. Where is this coming from?

I know Jenny as the little girl who used to cry
when she saw others being hurt, who laughed,
danced, gave hugs, and tended to her younger brother
in a tough family situation. Always caring, always
helping others. Her mother, my daughter, is battling
with alcohol, although she won't admit it. She's very
successful as a real estate agent, so she figures there's
no problem other than raising two kids alone. The father, a stockbroker, left when Jenny was two. There's
been no word since he remarried. Several other men
have come and gone. My daughter's a very pretty,
highly educated, confused lady. What did I do wrong?

Anyhow, that's how I got involved, taking in
Jenny and her brother sometimes when the pressure
was too much at home. It's been tough. I've tried to
set a good example, instilling and living by values,
morals. As a widow running my own business and
getting very little cooperation from Jenny's mother,
I'm afraid I didn't do enough. But all of this, the pregnancy, the fighting, falling grades, and the attitude toward authority, really began when she got tangled up
with Scott and his friends. A twenty-year-old man has
no business having sex with a fifteen-year-old girl. To
keep him away from her, I want to charge him with
statutory rape but Jenny threatens to run away if I do.
At any rate, he hasn't shown his face since the pregnancy, and Jenny will be staying with me on the Cape
for a while, visiting her mother on weekends. She
cries for Scott every night. What can I do?

What Nanna doesn't know is that her thoughtful, shy
granddaughter has broken into houses with Scott and his
friends, stolen cars, pawned hot goods, robbed and assaulted

other people. Jennifer's self-esteem and status, bolstered by Scott's praise and the group's acceptance, skyrocketed after every misguided test of loyalty and courage. Her violent attack on the girl who made a play for Scott was not an isolated incident. Furthermore, Nanna does not know the extent of the chaos and uncertainty in her granddaughter's home life, where rules and values are contradictory or arbitrary, where school is a chore that bears little relation to a more pressing reality. In Jennifer's world, Scott's attention is an elixir, a status symbol, and a guiding light.

LOOKING FOR CLUES

So what on earth went wrong with Zachary, the moralistic con, and Jennifer, the wayward teenager? Zachary seemed to have all the attributes, advantages, and tools needed to make his way through the world without hurting others, without resorting to crime. Jennifer's plight, on the other hand, is a bit more understandable. It appears that she has taken drastic, misguided measures to infuse her uncertain life with meaning, purpose, and structure. But how is she able to short-circuit the moral values that she learned from her grandmother? Clearly, she cares a great deal about people. But something went awry somewhere.

It would be easy but irresponsible to point to any single cause behind Zachary's or Jennifer's unethical behavior. Some might say that Zachary has an "antisocial personality disorder." That could be true but labeling it as such doesn't really help. A label is not an explanation and, in a way, dulls the edge of his responsibility. It implies that he is a victim of his disorder. Others might say that Zachary has strayed from the moral teachings of his family and church and needs to rekindle his faith. This could also be true, but such a view doesn't explain how or why he has taken this extreme detour.

Jennifer is caught in a familiar scenario involving a broken family, an absent father, alcohol abuse, erratic parenting, and a lack of direction. But so are a lot of good people. The vast majority don't rob others or slice up peers over petty arguments.

Jennifer is lost and very confused as her moral center fades from view. She now considers herself a "survivor," but the price has been high. She no longer feels like a good person.

Our concern here is to find out why Jennifer has such a tenuous grasp on her moral sense and why Zachary never seemed to develop one in the first place. We can't know all the answers, but we can look for clues in their upbringing. As we explore their lives (and the lives of Vanessa, Eric, David, and Shana), keep in mind that people bring different temperaments, strengths, and vulnerabilities to any particular situation. For example, Zachary's sister was raised in the same family, but she didn't become a criminal. And Jennifer's little brother may never join a criminal group or intentionally hurt anyone. A vast constellation of factors makes us who we are.

YOU GOT IT WRONG, SIGMUND

Sigmund Freud, that bearded king of psychoanalysis who invented such little gems as "penis envy," was responsible for many misconceptions about human nature. Some of these fallacies continue to haunt us today and influence how we raise our children.

In his view, you are fundamentally a selfish, sexual, aggressive ball of impulses precariously held in check by civilizing forces. You were born without a natural capacity to be kind, caring, or responsive to the pain of others. You have learned to pay attention to things like fairness and kindness only because it serves your best interests. Not enough self-control and you're likely to spew your impulses all over the place and alienate people. Too much control and you become neurotic. It's a rough job keeping the beast in line without making it crazy.

Well, okay. It may feel like that sometimes. All these things may be a part of our nature, but Sigmund's dramatic scenario tells us more about him and his time than it does the matter at hand. He didn't spend much time in the nursery. Two important qualities Sigmund overlooked were our inborn capacities for:

1. **Empathy**—our ability to experience the feelings of other people, their pain or their joy; and

2. **Altruism**—our desire to help others regardless of any rewards or punishments that might be involved. Altruism often follows from empathy.

Our concern here—the first step in figuring out what may have gone wrong with Zachary, Jennifer, and the others—centers on a very important fact: *We are born with varying degrees of empathy and its first cousin, altruism. Some of us are inherently more sensitive and giving than others. But each of these qualities can be enhanced with learning.* Let's take a closer look at empathy and see how it applies to our stories.

FEELING THE PAIN OF OTHERS

If you happen to be watching as your good friend slices himself while shaving, chances are you'll cringe and skew your face in distress. You may even dab his bleeding wound with tissue. If he gets dumped by his girlfriend and falls into despair, you'll probably feel his anxiety in the pit of your stomach and his sadness in your heart. You might be moved to share your own painful experiences with lost loves and offer encouragement and advice. If you're the reason his girlfriend dumped him, you'll probably be fending off your own demons of guilt. Your guilt can feel as powerful and debilitating as your friend's despair. Even more amazing, you may be moved to tears by the plight of a stranger or a fictional character. If you don't experience at least some of these reactions, something is terribly wrong.

Empathy lies at the core of our moral development. The capacity to place ourselves in the other person's shoes forms the basis of our motivation to be kind and caring. We know what it feels like to hurt. For most people, the first spark of empathy just happens. In the examples above, you don't consciously decide to feel your friend's pain. It's almost automatic, even though you may attempt to block or numb out the feeling.

In some instances, however, you may need to make an effort to trigger or revive your empathy. This happens most often when you can't identify with those in pain, or when another emotion, such as anger, gets in the way. Think of your feeling when the gamy guy on the street duns you for change as he swills the Night Train. Or think of the last time you hurled painful barbs at a well-meaning loved one. As you will see in chapters 5 and 6, human beings have devised all sorts of mind games to avoid or downplay empathy. These games can be useful at times, but they're extremely dangerous to play. We see the consequences every night on the news.

Where Empathy Comes From

Ask any observant parent. Many newborn infants, weeks or even days old, can tell the difference between the smiling face of a pleased parent and the serious expression of a worried one. They sense changes in mood and respond differently. If they hear another infant crying, they're likely to cry also. Try to fool them by imitating a baby's cry and they'll just stare at you. They know the real thing. This sensitivity to another's distress is the beginning of empathy. At this point, however, infants can't put together the feelings and the reasons for them. They just are.

By age two, most children are beginning to figure out the causes of their own feelings and the feelings of others. They know they're afraid or sad because Mommy's gone. And they may know that Mommy's unhappy because Daddy yelled at her. At this point, it is not uncommon for a child to offer comfort to a distressed parent, often in the form of a cookie, stuffed animal, pacifier, or blanket. If Mommy feels better, the child will feel better. Comforting others feels good, while harming them feels bad. Guilt is possible. This emotional connection sets the stage for further moral development.

By age four or five, most children are aware of many more feelings, in themselves and others, and why they have occurred. They are increasingly able to take the other person's perspective: "Some things that make me feel good don't make you feel good." They are beginning to see that people have needs and desires that may be different from their own. They're learning how to make others feel better. Perspective-taking like this is essential for *moral sensitivity,* which is our ability to see that many of our actions, however benign they may seem to us, have the power to help or hurt others. Perspective-taking depends upon reasoning ability, which continues to improve as children develop. More on this later.

Between the ages of ten and twelve, children make another important transition in the development of empathy. Up to this point, most of their concerns and feelings have been focused on situations they've directly experienced or seen. But now, something different begins to emerge. Children become more sensitive to the pain and suffering of people in general, just by using their imagination and empathy. They can feel for those less fortunate than themselves, even though they have had no direct involvement with them. This is an important step toward social awareness and acting for the common good.

Why Empathy Fails to Develop Fully

There are many, many ways in which this can happen. Most involve failures in the child-parent bond, emotional and physical abuse, erratic and inconsistent parenting, poor role modeling, and failures in emotional guidance. In most cases, a combination of these factors is at work. But the child's inborn capacity for empathy, along with other personality features, is also part of the equation. Quite remarkably, some children grow into kind, considerate adults in spite of major parental failures.

Let's look at a few examples, followed by some important tips for nurturing empathy. Keep in mind that the equation and the results vary with different children.

Difficult Babies, Distant Parents: Tenuous Bonds

Zachary, the mail fraud schemer described at the beginning of this chapter, seems to experience kernels of compassion here and there, particularly toward those he considers less fortunate:

> I like helping people, always have. It makes me happy to know that I have the power and money to do it. And their gratitude makes me feel good. Sometimes I feel like Robin Hood, taking from the rich, giving to the poor. But I really had no intention of keeping the money from the foundation thing. I was moving it around to solve some cash flow problems when the authorities moved in. They misread the situation, so here I am.

Zachary does have a capacity for empathy, but it is limited and superficial. When he does feel empathy, it is easily squashed by selfish motives. Much of the time, he only acts *as if* he feels empathy. He reads people like a master, but his own feelings often don't resonate with the vibes he stirs up. He knows what's expected of him and goes through the motions, unaware that something important is lacking. Zachary uses people and always has a good explanation for his actions. His mother describes parts of his childhood:

> Zach was a very different baby from Kathy, his older sister. Kathy loved to be cuddled and calmed down immediately when I caressed her. Zach would scream and holler, no matter what. His cry was piercing. It took great patience to deal with him, and sometimes I just threw him in his father's lap. His father, of course, couldn't do anything. To him, babies were alien creatures.
>
> He was demanding and irritable as a young child. We had him evaluated for hyperactivity but nothing was found. His nursery school teacher and his doctor

said that Zach wasn't really a problem. He calmed down easily when he wanted to. But he wasn't quite so docile with us.

Things didn't get better at home until we began teaching and enforcing strict guidelines about right and wrong. His father was very helpful with this. I would fall into the trap of always explaining everything to Zach. His father would say, "Do it because I say so, or else," which seemed to work. Zach did very well until he was out on his own.

As any parent knows, children in the same family can vary widely in temperament and in their sensitivity to the feelings of other people. Zachary's irritable temperament, his annoying cry, and his low level of responsiveness made him a particularly difficult infant to coddle. This can be disconcerting for any parent. Zachary's mother felt rejected, hurt, and defeated. This in turn caused her to pull away even more. A bond of empathy was formed, but it never fully developed. Furthermore, neither she nor her husband knew about the very specific ways in which they might have been able to enhance empathy in this difficult child. We'll look at some of these methods later.

Zachary's problem with empathy is only part of the picture. Later on, you'll see why he was unable to use and apply the moral values so thoroughly instilled by his well-meaning parents.

As Reliable as the Wind: Erratic Parenting

Jennifer, the fifteen-year-old involved in delinquent, sometimes violent behavior, is different from Zachary. She has a much greater capacity to genuinely feel for others. Nevertheless, some of the cruelties she commits are far more direct and bone-chilling than Zachary's deceits. She sees the painful grimacing of those she assaults, yet she continues. How does she do it? Quite simply, she turns her empathy on and off like a switch. She's been practicing for years. Jennifer's grandmother provides a few clues about her early development:

> She was a peach, the cutest baby in the world. Her mother loved her so much, wouldn't put her down. She treated Jenny as if her own life depended upon it. But that was before the marriage broke up. Shortly afterward, I remember driving all the way up from the Cape to find her mother passed out on the couch, inebriated. Little Jenny couldn't have been much more than two. Having been left alone for hours, she ran to me and held on. I didn't want to let go but I had no right to take her away. Her mother said it was a terrible mistake, that she was depressed about her divorce, that it wouldn't happen again. But I'm sure it did. Should I have reported my own daughter for child neglect? I don't know.
>
> I don't believe Jenny was ever hit, but her mother would suddenly turn on her, criticize her for no reason. She'd tell Jenny to do this or that, then yell at her for doing it. When drinking, my daughter would get into terrible moods—all lovey one moment, irritable and explosive the next. I'll never forget the look on Jenny's face, like the earth opened up and swallowed her. But after a while, it was as if she got used to it and would just stare. She seemed like such a strong child in so many respects, taking care of her brother, tending to the daily tasks that her mother often ignored. I guess it was too much.

Jennifer's strong capacity for empathy was damaged along the way by her mother's erratic behavior. She was loved one moment, then, for no discernible reason, hurt and rejected the next. Nothing made sense, least of all her mother's feelings and reactions. And Jennifer couldn't do anything to make the situation better. She quickly learned to selectively numb her sense of shame, rage, and empathy. She's heading for some agonizing emotional problems.

Lousy Role Models, Poor Training

While the love and guidance that Jennifer received were erratic, inconsistent, and confusing, Eric grew up in a world where love meant rescuing his mother and placating his father. Eric, as you may remember from his story in chapter 1 (beginning on page 7), is the twenty-six-year-old assistant store manager who was abused by his father and now abuses his wife, Vanessa. As a child, the level of guidance Eric received from either parent was superficial and grossly inadequate. His abusive father was overbearing, controlling, and rigid. The only emotions that counted were his own. Feelings simply were not discussed—they were ridiculed. Eric began to associate emotions with his mother, whom he perceived as passive, weak, and suffocating.

> My mother never stood up to him. I don't really blame her, because I couldn't do it either. We tried to protect each other. It's like we were both kids. I'd talked to her but she couldn't even handle her own problems. It's like, since I was the male, I was the one who was supposed to get us out of the mess. I got sick of her disgusting whining. Sometimes it feels the same way when Vanessa hangs on me.

Eric's father criticized and lectured him on right and wrong but never explained the reasoning behind his exhortations. Eric was forced to accept conclusions without question. If he tried to raise concerns, express new ideas, or be different from his father, explosions inevitably followed. He was convinced that his father didn't really care about his thoughts or feelings. In spite of this, he wanted to be like his powerful father—anything to avoid the shame and humiliation of being weak and dependent like his mother.

Eric was expected to read his father's mind, and in a way became quite good at it. But that's the only wavelength he picked up. That's where his sensitivity ended. And like many people immersed in trauma, Eric became preoccupied and self-absorbed. Now, when confronted with the subtle needs of other people, Eric fails miserably. Just like his father, he expects others to feel as he does. Aside from the emotional numbing, Eric's moral sensitivity and empathy have been stifled by his inability to understand others. His *perspective-taking* has not been fully developed. For all he knows, your shoes feel the same as his.

Vanessa, Eric's twenty-four-year-old wife, has the opposite problem. In many ways, she actually has *too much* empathy. She's the eternal rescuer, the woman who "loves too much." She blames herself when things go wrong, allows Eric to take advantage of her, and builds him up at her own expense. Vanessa is very much like her mother—submissive and deferential to her husband's needs. Her own feelings don't count.

I could go on and on about failures and complications in the development of empathy, but I think you get the point. If you're a parent or want to spot possible lapses in your own upbringing, the most important information is found in the following Benchmark.

BENCHMARK NO. 2
THE BEST WAYS TO NURTURE EMPATHY

1. Treat your child with love, affection, kindness, consideration, and respect. Her positive bond with you will form the building blocks for empathy and moral sensitivity. The bond is also vital for the development of your authority as a parent. This will be important as you set standards of behavior for your child.

2. Show her that you understand her needs and feelings. Help her put them into words.

3. Let her know that you care about the feelings of other people, both by your actions and your words.

4. If she does something inconsiderate or hurtful to you, tell her how it makes you feel, and explain why. Help her find a more considerate approach. Show approval when she is considerate.

5. Help her tune in to the feelings of other people. Explain how someone might feel in a certain situation and why.

6. Encourage her to take another perspective, to place herself in the other person's shoes and imagine how she might feel. To help her understand and connect to the feeling, point out similar situations in her life.

7. When she helps others and considers their needs, emphasize how good it makes her feel.

8. Whenever she feels as if she wants to hurt someone, emphasize self-control. Help her understand why she might feel that way. Have her imagine what the other person might be feeling.

9. Point out and praise empathetic, altruistic acts carried out by other people.

10. Don't just resort to a list of dos and don'ts when it comes to the treatment of other people. Your exhortations will only have sustainable power if you explain the reasoning behind them.

(For a more detailed look at building empathy in children, I highly recommend *Bringing Up a Moral Child,* by Michael Schulman and Eva Mekler, Addison-Wesley Publishing, 1985. Many points on this list were adapted from their research.)

THE OUGHTS AND THE SHALL-NOTS

When Zachary, our moralistic con man, set up his phony foundation to defraud the elderly, he knew it was wrong, but he didn't feel much of anything. His inner voice was harsh, but it rolled off his back. Another voice, aimed at his father, took over. *Look, get off my case. You can't control me anymore, don't you understand? If I don't do this, someone else will. Nobody's really getting hurt. These people have money and it makes them feel good to donate to a worthy cause. I have to get something for my trouble, don't I? Your corporation screwed people, so don't give me grief.*

When David, the married attorney described in chapter 1 (see page 12), first contemplated an affair with Shana, his young legal assistant, his stomach balled up and his palms broke out in a sweat. He could hardly eat for a week. But it wasn't the anticipation of a sexual extravaganza that depressed his appetite. The inner voice in his head simply wouldn't give him a break. *You're an idiot. This isn't right and you know it. You can't cheat on Noreen. What's more important—your testosterone or your family? You can't hurt them. You're not that kind of guy. Would your father have done this to your mother? No way!*

When fifteen-year-old Jennifer and her older boyfriend Scott broke into houses or stole cars, her head was filled with something different. *This really takes guts. It feels so great to do anything I want and not worry about it. Scott loves it, the adrenaline rush. He even brags about me, how I don't cop out. He says he's proud to be with me.*

Three people, three different inner voices. Zachary is still waging an inner battle against his strong-minded father. His father, you may remember, lectured him constantly about right and wrong, hoping to instill some values in his rather difficult child. But they didn't really stick. Zachary knew the words but not the feelings. David, on the other hand, is thrown into turmoil because his extramarital affair with Shana violates the basic values that he holds dear. Many of these values are holdovers from childhood, but David sees them as his own. They don't feel like moral injunctions imposed by parents. And young Jennifer suspends her fragile values to please her older boyfriend.

What we're talking about here, of course, is *conscience.* Conscience—the inner voice—involves self-control and the adherence to certain moral standards. It lets us know when we've strayed from our values. How is our conscience developed and why does it differ so much from person to person?

Where Conscience Comes From

Long before David dreamed of becoming an attorney or even imagined the temptations of sex, the seeds of conscience were germinating. When David was two years old, he grabbed a handful of crayons and decorated the living room wall. His mother shrieked at the sight, eyes afire and fists clenched. "My God, Davey, what have you done? No! No! That's bad!" Her anger lasted only a few seconds, but for David it seemed as if his world were over. Quickly calming down and containing her impulse to throttle the budding artist, David's mother carefully explained that crayons are for drawing on paper, not walls. Crayons damage walls. He cried, said he was sorry, and buried himself in her arms. He never wrote on the walls again.

The rule was simple, but David learned it well. He loved his mother very much and felt terrible that he had displeased her. He felt ashamed and guilty that he had been bad. He knew he would get into trouble if he ever did it again, but even more important, he didn't want to lose his mother's approval and love. He wanted to be good, to make her happy.

For the first few years of David's life, his ideas about good and bad behavior depended very much upon his parents' expectations and responses. The power behind this was the love they shared, something David did not want to lose. Whenever he started to do something selfish, destructive, or hurtful, he would remember his parents' rules and envision their disapproval. Since the rules and expectations were clear, and the *reasons* behind them spelled out, David soon took them on as his own. The rules and values became part of his conscience. Most of them simply made good sense. And he felt good about himself when they were followed.

So, in a nutshell, that's how rules and values become deeply ingrained as conscience. Love, bonding, empathy, and reasoning are crucial ingredients. Punishment, lectures, and coercion alone totally miss the boat and are apt to produce a child who lacks self-regulation. Values imposed in this manner remain on the surface and feel as if they belong to someone else.

You saw some degree of this problem in Zachary, the slippery schemer. His father was well-meaning but distant and extremely strict. Communication was basically in one direction. As soon as Zachary left his parents' control, he reverted to immature, hurtful behavior. His conscience was something to fight rather than follow.

How Parenting Styles May Affect Conscience

This brings us to some important but sticky concerns and opinions regarding punishment, permissiveness, communication, and parenting styles in general. You've heard the arguments before from politicians and others expounding on our moral demise: Parents are too lenient, inconsistent, ignorant of moral values, unavailable, and unconcerned. They need to get tough, teach basic values, and provide firm consequences.

While this is certainly true in many cases, it's a simplistic solution to a complex problem. Finding the right balance of parental authority, punishment, and permissiveness can be a wrenching process for any parent.

For some general guidelines, let's look at four different parenting styles and how they might affect a child's budding conscience and value system. Keep in mind that although parents may have a predominant style, the day-to-day style often varies with the situation and the child. For example, a father who is overwhelmed at work may become short-tempered and harsh until the stress lets up. A mother may be lenient with her son but strict and rigid with her daughter.

Style No. 1: The Authoritarian Parent

- The parent is invested in strict control, with very little two-way communication about family rules and decision making. Children aren't allowed much voice. The family is run more like a dictatorship than a democracy. The reasons behind the rules and values are not clearly discussed. "Do it because I say so" is the extent of the communication in nearly all situations.

- The parent is likely to be highly punitive, with the main parenting efforts aimed at enforcing punishment after a breach has been committed. The focus is on setting limits.

- The parent usually avoids getting too close to the kids. Warmth and nurturance are not strong points.

- Such a parent may discipline the child in ways that are coercive, harsh, or inconsistent, depending upon the parent's mood.

- The parent's expectations are unrealistic. Socially mature behavior is expected from kids regardless of age and development.

- Because the parent is so controlling and intrusive, the kids' development may be thwarted. They are not free to make their own mistakes or experience the stress of having to make difficult decisions.

- The authoritarian parent often ends up raising children who lack assertiveness, self-reliance, and an inner sense of responsibility. The children may have a limited ability to handle setbacks, and their sense of social responsibility is likely to be stunted. Their conscience is not their own.

Style No. 2: The Overindulgent Parent

- The parent is basically permissive and takes very little control. Warmth and nurturance are stressed.

- The parent communicates openly, with frequent discussions. The family style is basically democratic.

- Unfortunately, the parent fails to confront the children firmly enough when they've gone astray. The message often doesn't sink in. Uncomfortable in an authoritarian role, the parent avoids making mature demands of the children.

- The parent, as a rule, is overprotective, and fails to enforce rules and to punish delinquencies. Like the authoritarian parent, this parent stifles a child's development. The child, protected from hurtful feelings, often fails to grasp the realistic consequences of his or her behavior. The parent, zealous to protect the child, may interfere with the legitimate expression of authority by teachers, police, and other institutions.

- Even though kind and caring, the overindulgent parent usurps the kid's sense of responsibility. The potential effects are similar to those seen with authoritarian parents—lack of self-control, cruel behavior, and disobedience. Conscience is not firmly established.

Style No. 3: The Self-Involved Parent

- The parent is lenient, like the overindulgent parent, but harsh and punitive like the authoritarian. In other words, they are grossly inconsistent.

- Most of the time, the parent is lenient, permissive, and generally unconcerned. Due to a high level of self-involvement, not much effort is made to guide the children. Rules are arbitrarily enforced, and the kids are not consistently held accountable.

- However, all hell breaks loose if a child happens to do anything which directly imposes upon or disturbs the parent. Talking back, making too much noise, not helping with the chores, embarrassing the parent, and so forth, are often met with severe punishment. The message is "how dare you do this to me."

- The self-involved parent is likely to raise children who are very aggressive and confused, and lack a moral center. Conscience in these children can be very tenuous.

Style No. 4: The Well-Balanced Parent

- The parent practices a style which combines firm parental control with a democratic-like environment. Children have a voice but the parent remains in charge.

- The well-balanced parent keeps communication clear and honest. The reasoning behind a value or rule is openly discussed. Expectations are clear. Deception and manipulation are avoided.

- While warm and caring, the parent remains firm and consistent. There is no fear of strongly confronting the children or enforcing parental commands.

- The parent is demanding yet sensitive to the capabilities of each child. Realistic challenges are imposed to help each child mature.

- A sense of responsibility toward legitimate authority is instilled and modeled by the parent. At the same time, the parent encourages questions concerning the rationale behind the authority.

- The well-balanced parent often raises children who are more likely to be kind, assertive, friendly, respectful, and responsible. The children have an internal set of guidelines that survives the direct intervention of their parent. Conscience is more fully developed in these children.

Most certainly, parenting styles don't always fit neatly into these four categories. Parents may fall in and out of, or combine, various styles according to life's demands and their own emotional stability. Or, heaven forbid, each parent may have a drastically different style. Family therapists and divorce lawyers get rich handling those cases. But regardless of all the possible variations, a certain atmosphere usually predominates in each family.

(For an in-depth look at parenting styles and moral development, I highly recommend *The Moral Child: Nurturing Children's Natural Moral Growth,* by William Damon, Free Press, 1988.)

Parenting Styles and Conscience in Action

Eric, the assistant retail manager who abuses his wife, Vanessa, was raised in an authoritarian atmosphere that deteriorated into harsh, arbitrary physical punishment. His father, you may remember, was physically abusive and emotionally cruel to Eric and the entire family. Although Eric's mother was generally overindulgent in her style, his father's authoritarian style dominated the family. Zachary, the mail fraud schemer, also grew up in an authoritarian family, although it was much more sophisticated and values-oriented than Eric's. Eric got little if any guidance, while Zachary was hit over the head with it.

The net effect of these parenting styles on conscience, however, was quite similar for both men. Both Eric and Zachary, to varying degrees, have a stunted sense of personal responsibility and live as if they are constantly fighting *against* the world, against external rules and regulations. They always find reasons and justifications for their actions, and manage to head off shame and guilt at the pass.

Jennifer, the fifteen-year-old girl with the alcoholic mother, grew up with a mixture of approaches. Her grandmother, the widow who owns a pastry shop on Cape Cod, was consistent and presented a fairly well-balanced approach, but she wasn't always available. Jennifer's alcoholic mother, grossly erratic and self-involved, worked long, unpredictable hours as a real estate agent. She provided very little guidance and tended to respond only when Jennifer got in the way of her needs. Jennifer never knew what to expect and soon learned to shut everything out. In many ways, she assumed the role of parent, for herself and her younger brother.

While Jennifer did indeed develop a conscience, it was rather diffuse and tenuous, without a strong center. Although the moral glue of her conscience may have been sufficiently strong for the demands of childhood, the additional pressures of adolescence brought on confusion, loss of direction, and an explosive sense of frustration. She had few resources to rely upon consistently. Her conscience was easily overwhelmed by more immediate emotional needs and external forces.

Shana, David's legal assistant and twenty-seven-year-old mistress, was raised by an overindulgent stepfather and a self-involved, somewhat authoritarian mother. Shana's stepfather was a long-distance truck driver who showered his beautiful stepdaughter with insincere praise and affection, regardless of her behavior. Since he was seldom home, he had little hand in discipline and soon became idealized in Shana's eyes. He was good, while her distant, preoccupied mother was bad. Her mother, a licensed practical nurse, was depressed much of the time and had little energy to handle her vivacious child. She made and enforced rules arbitrarily, according to her own needs.

Shana's life with her depressed mother was devoid of love and approval unless she performed exactly to her mother's expectations. She often felt empty and manipulated, like a plastic doll. Her mother seemed to have no sense of Shana's needs and feelings as a separate human being. The only thing that really filled Shana's void was her stepfather's attention. But this became quite complex when he slipped into her room one night and taught her secret pleasures. Shana was terribly ashamed but ecstatic at the same time. For the first time in her life, she felt alive, important, and powerful. Her emptiness was filled, at least temporarily.

While Shana may have been born with certain traits and tendencies, her upbringing has had a drastic effect on her developing personality structure, her conscience, and her moral sense. She experiences immense guilt at times, but it is quickly diminished as she consciously and unconsciously twists situations to avoid moral responsibility. Her vision is littered with blind spots and she flip-flops on moral issues at the drop of a hat. At one moment, she is the eternal victim who rationalizes her behavior and blames others. At the next, she blames herself for everything, as if there were no boundaries in the world.

Shana's relationships lack depth because she was never fully loved in the first place. Although she is capable of empathy, particularly toward children and animals, her understanding of other adults is limited. Her tendency is to place people into either good or bad categories; shades of gray are too hard to handle. You'll see the full extent of Shana's moral and psychological confusion in future chapters. Her difficulties go beyond the realm of a poorly developed conscience.

Important Tips

Before looking at another vital aspect of moral development, here's a Benchmark of suggestions for instilling a healthy conscience in young children. As in all phases of human development, love, bonding, empathy, and reasoning are crucial here. These ingredients, along with respect for parental authority, set the stage for the child's successful participation in society.

BENCHMARK NO. 3

CREATING A HEALTHY CONSCIENCE

1. Work to develop a secure, loving relationship with your child. Without it, your efforts will be seriously handicapped.

2. Make sure that rules are very specific and clearly spelled out.

3. Explain the rationale behind rules. Explain how breaking the rule in question might affect other people. Use concrete examples. This encourages learning and thinking rather than blind obedience.

4. Don't dodge questions about the "fairness" of rules. Help your child to think through issues of fairness. For example, he may want to know why his sister or a friend doesn't have to follow the same rule. Try not to give simplistic explanations—"This is something that all good boys do."

5. Always confront your child if his or her actions might harm others.

6. Consistently enforce your commands. Be direct and honest, not manipulative,

7. Use as little force or coercion as necessary to bring about compliance, but be sure that you get your point across. Too little force and your message might not stick. Too much and your child will remember the force and forget your message.

8. Let your child know what's expected and what the consequences will be if the rules are breached. But don't expect more than he or she is capable of.

9. Be a good model of authority and be respectful of other legitimate authority. Demonstrate that authority can be questioned in a civilized manner.

10. Don't turn everything into a moral issue. Overdoing it stifles and confuses kids. Behavior that doesn't really hurt others can be handled without invoking shame or guilt.

THINKING THINGS THROUGH

Our conscience is made up of values that have been instilled by others as well as values that we've *chosen* for ourselves. After all, we're not simply clones of our parents. As we mature, we usually reject those values that don't seem to work or make sense. We also acquire new values. How do we do this? And how do we weigh and sort through all the conflicting values when we're faced with a moral dilemma? Empathy and conscience alone aren't enough.

The Importance of Moral Reasoning

This brings us to another key ingredient in moral development. As we attempt to see all sides of a difficult moral dilemma, the values at stake, and the rights and needs of others, we must use our moral reasoning to determine what we *ought* to do. Moral reasoning refers to our capacity to understand *why* some actions may be morally better than others. This capacity generally changes as we mature. Our perspective broadens and our priorities change.

For example, if we ask a seven-year-old why it's wrong to steal, he's likely to say, "It's not good to steal because you get in trouble" or "If you steal from someone, they might steal from you." His focus is limited to himself and the immediate consequences. Ask a mature teenager the same question and she might say, "It's wrong. If everybody went around stealing, society would fall apart."

While the seven-year-old's moral reasoning is indeed correct, the teenager's thinking is more developed. For her, the reasoning goes beyond punishment or tit-for-tat consequences. She sees that the act of stealing has implications that are larger than her own immediate needs. She understands that a certain level of social cooperation is necessary in a civilized society. (Whether she actually practices what she preaches is another story entirely. See chapter 10.)

Our moral reasoning develops as our perspective broadens. And our perspective broadens as we learn the reasons behind values, experience the give-and-take of successful relationships, place ourselves in other people's shoes, and think through moral conflicts. We began to truly understand why certain values, such as the Incredible Seven described on page 28 (fairness, caring, respect, responsibility, honesty, loyalty, and liberty) are helpful. Likewise, we are able to give some values priority over others. We begin to understand why we must look beyond ourselves to family, society, and human rights in general.

However, if we make little attempt to navigate the moral maze or if we live by moral rhetoric alone, our moral reasoning is likely to stagnate at a certain level, or even regress. Some people, in spite of obvious intelligence, never really grow beyond the moral reasoning level of the seven-year-old cited on page 64. They fail to get the larger picture. Others have major gaps in the development of their moral reasoning and regress in self-serving situations. You'll see other examples in chapter 9, along with guidelines for identifying the various levels of moral reasoning.

GET REAL!

Okay, you say, this is all well and good. But I know people who are warm and caring, eat themselves alive with guilt, have an overgrown social conscience—all the good stuff you're talking about. And they still might rip off other people, beat their partners, take unfair advantage, lie, cheat, deal cocaine— you name it, they do it. Even murder. Explain that, wise guy.

Good point. Things can really get out of whack, even when you've grown up with decent, loving parents. We've all seen well-known, respected individuals fail in some area of their lives. And perhaps you've had your own ups and downs, in spite of good intentions. How does this happen?

FOUR

Shocking Truths, or "I Can't Believe He Would Do Such a Thing!"

So many good people—partners we've loved, friends we've trusted, politicians we've respected, and heroes we've admired. So many slip-ups, slow tumbles, or nosedives from grace. And unless you've lived in a cave all your life, you can probably include yourself on that list. No one gets through unscathed.

The slip-ups and the slow tumbles are the easiest to understand. We all make mistakes: Your best friend breaks a confidence; your sister-in-law, in a moment of anger, says hurtful things behind your back; your frazzled boss uses you as a scapegoat, and so forth. Chances are, you're not totally shocked, because you have a fairly good idea about the other person's character and personality. Or at least you think you do.

But what about the nosedives? What if you find out that your trusted accountant is embezzling money and your best friend, Joe the Cop, deals drugs on the job? Or that your favorite cousin had the beloved family dog put to sleep because he chewed a shoe? What now? Since most of us need to see ourselves and those we admire as good people, we're radically thrown when that picture is cracked or shattered. This is particularly true when the harmful behavior appears to be senseless or totally out of character. "I simply can't believe he would do such a thing. I've been his close friend for years!"

Looking for explanations, perhaps we attribute the behavior to stress, inescapable circumstances, a lousy childhood, self-deception, a psychotic break, or some sort of psychological syndrome. One or more of these psychological factors could certainly be a large part of the equation. They are discussed throughout this book.

But there is another factor that we tend to overlook, particularly when we have a vested interest in liking the transgressor. I'm talking about the weakness or lapse in *character* that allowed the behavior to occur in the first place, regardless of the other influences. We all have lapses, but for some individuals the behavior is so terrible and unexpected that we begin to wonder if we really knew that person at all. Perhaps there is a side to his or her character that we never saw. Why didn't we see it, and how do we explain the inconsistencies? Even more important, how do we keep our own character in balance?

CHARACTER AND VALUES

How can a warm, caring, responsible father secretly moonlight as a hitman? His unknowing children think he is wonderful. How can a politician devote enormous time and energy to his country while totally neglecting his suffering family? His constituents know him as courageous and hardworking. How can a respected sports hero brutalize his beautiful wife? His fans see him as totally charming and honorable. To understand these contradictions, we need to look more closely at "character."

What do we mean when we talk about someone's character? Quite simply, character is our "moral personality." It's intimately related to our psychological personality, but it also includes the moral values we hold and apply. These values reflect how we wish to treat other people, as well as the personal virtues that we might aspire to, such as self-discipline, courage, integrity, tolerance, and so forth. In short, *good character is the side of our personality that is concerned with doing the right thing.* We'll look at all the components of good character in chapter 10. But for now, our concern centers on the important role values play in character, how values get out of whack, and how we lose ourselves in the shuffle.

Warning: Pigeonholes and Jelly Beans

Before going any further, a word to the wise. When we talk about someone's personality or character, we often make it sound as if it's a permanent, stable fixture attached to the body, like a hand or a foot. And when we have to size it up, we frequently resort to very broad impressions and descriptive categories based on a few casual observations. "He's been a good neighbor, a decent guy, quiet, always helpful, considerate, easy to be around." Since he seems to like you, you're more apt to view him favorably. A really great guy. You might even be happy to give him a character reference.

It was reported many years ago that Ronald Reagan sized up personality with a jelly bean test. He'd offer visitors candy from a jar and observe their responses. Some took one bean, some politely refused, some chose beans of one color, others were less discriminating. Some chewed, while others sucked slowly. The nuances of interpretation were left to our highly bemused chief executive. Thus went the fate of the nation.

We all have a natural tendency to think in broad categories (a "slow sucker"), using the scantiest of evidence (three beans in ten minutes), while overlooking alternative explanations (he had just eaten three Big Macs). We then treat the categories as tangible "things" to be measured, prodded, and picked over. That's the way we organize and structure input from perceptions. But that's also how we oversimplify, mislabel, and pigeonhole people.

We're liberals or conservatives, Capricorns or Leos, radical feminists or neofeminists, Volvo drivers or BMW yuppies, good guys or bad guys, us or them—all sorts of simplistic categories that may influence our attitude toward others as well as our self-image. The categories may have

some accuracy on the superficial level, but we can't automatically assume that the details will hold true. Yet we fall
into this trap constantly because broad categories are quick,
easy, and serve our beliefs and expectations. You may want
and need the neighbor to be an all around "good guy" because you like each other.

But using a broad brush to paint portraits of our fellow
human beings may produce some real surprises, for better or
worse. The fact of the matter is, a person may have *many* different faces and levels of personality and character, some of
which don't become evident until a particular situation or
role arises. Ronald Reagan, of all people, should have known
better.

PRIVATE FACES, PUBLIC ROLES

To understand how character and values contribute to the
major nosedives from grace, it's helpful to look at yourself.
You undoubtedly have a general sense of the person you are.
But the picture is likely to change as you face different situations and assume various roles—with intimates, family
members, good friends, employers, community members,
and society in general. For example, you may be a dynamic,
assertive person at work but passive and lazy at home. You
may be fearful and shy in general but courageous when a
loved one is threatened. You may be argumentative and defensive around your parents but mature and levelheaded
around your spouse. You may be a relentless killer in war
but a gentle soul at home. Or, you may change very little.

The same discrepancies and variations may hold true for
certain aspects of your character. Character, remember, is
your "moral personality." It includes the values that you aspire to. Although you may not be fully aware of it, the values you choose to emphasize, downplay, or disregard are
likely to change depending upon the particular level of social interaction you're addressing. You may be highly responsible to your family but lackadaisical at work. You may

strive to be fair with others but accept unfair treatment for yourself. You may treat your friends and your boss with respect but constantly degrade your spouse.

Most people have at least eight social levels in which they play out different aspects of their character, including their moral values:

1. Self
2. Intimate relationships
3. Immediate and extended family
4. Friends
5. Job
6. Community
7. Country
8. Society in general

Ideally, your values should be fairly consistent and well balanced across the levels. But no one is perfect, and situations can demand uncomfortable compromises. Unfortunately, it's all too easy for values on one or more levels to stagnate, distort in small, almost unnoticeable increments, or go completely haywire. This can have major implications for your self-image and your mental health, not to mention the people your actions affect. Think about how you felt the last time you had to do something at work that violated your standards. Or think about the people who were affected by the devoted Nazi fathers.

When values remain undeveloped, change too radically, or grossly contradict each other from level to level, a whole array of psychological and relationship problems can result. Guilt, anxiety, depression, and identity confusion are common. This can happen to any of us, to varying degrees. In the extreme, if we are totally blind to the moral inconsistencies in our lives or choose to ignore them, sooner or later we pay the price. Just ask someone like O.J. Simpson, the respected sports hero accused of murdering his wife. Whether he's guilty or not, his abusive behavior on the intimate level of his life eventually led to his undoing. For O.J. and for all of us, the social and psychological consequences of our inconsistencies may come back to haunt us, causing our behavior to deteriorate even further in a negative, self-perpetuating cycle. Chances are, the people who shock us with unseemly acts have been building such a negative cycle for years. How can we make sure it doesn't happen to us?

TUNING UP YOUR VALUES PROFILE

Even if we don't commit major moral breaches, it's easy for our values to get out of whack across the different levels of our complicated lives. The discrepancies can compromise character, impede development, and diminish the quality of our lives. As a first step toward a better balance, we should at least be *aware* when we are operating by different standards in different situations. We can do this by periodically running a *Values Profile.* A values profile, as you saw briefly in chapter 1, is an informal snapshot of how a person relates to the world in a moral sense. It covers each of the levels of interaction described above (self, intimate relationships, family, friends, job, community, country, and society in general) and examines the values followed or aspired to on each level. Let's take a more detailed look at how a Values Profile works.

Back in chapter 1, you saw how Eric and Vanessa, the young couple involved in a physically and emotionally abusive relationship, had both ignored the moral implications of their situation. Eric refused to accept responsiblity for his explosive tantrums and Vanessa made excuses for him. Although afraid, she saw no reason to confront him or leave. Both partners downplayed the harmful effects of this environment on Eddie, their two-year-old son. Eric himself grew up with an abusive, controlling father, and now, at age twenty-six, continues to harbor a deep but unacknowledged sense of shame and personal weakness. Vanessa, his wife of three years, is the woman who "loves too much," the eternal rescuer.

As a guide for evaluating their situation, we relied on some key values, the Incredible Seven (justice and fairness, caring, respect, responsibility, honesty, loyalty, and liberty). (You'll find a discussion of the Incredible Seven, along with definitions, on page 28). The Incredible Seven values are broad-based and generally "good" for interpersonal relationships. Although we can argue about semantics, exact definitions, and whether other values should be included, most of us would like to be treated with these key values in mind.

Using these values, we looked at Eric and Vanessa in turn, seeing just how far each had strayed from the ideal. In the context of their relationship, Eric violated nearly every one of the Incredible Seven. Vanessa, the "victim" here, allowed herself to be treated unfairly, was less than honest about the situation, and failed to act responsibly in not protecting their son.

Notice that I said Eric's violations occurred "in the context of their relationship." What I'm really talking about here is his application of values on level 2—intimate relationships. Whenever issues of intimacy and love creep into Eric's life, immense psychological and moral problems are triggered. He becomes a defensive, controlling, abusive, but needy tyrant who tramples on principles of humane treatment, fairness, respect, and honesty. We can learn a lot about Eric by looking at his Values Profile across the social levels.

Eric's Values Profile

As we follow Eric through the eight levels of social interaction, a slightly different picture begins to emerge on each level. As he moves away from intimate relationships, he is increasingly able and willing to apply the Incredible Seven, at least up to a certain point. Nevertheless, there are major lapses along the way, and his level of social involvement doesn't go much further than his job. There are strengths as well as weaknesses.

1. *Self:* Extremely self-involved, dishonest, little self-respect, inadequate. Ashamed.

2. *Intimate Relationships:* Breaks down in all values, even though he can be caring and respectful for several days or weeks after a blowup.

3. *Immediate and Extended Family:* Caring and generally kind toward son. But irresponsible toward his immediate family as a unit. Places them at great risk. Breaks promises, not particularly loyal. Doesn't really get involved with extended family. Dishonest. Lies to them about his marriage. Has façade as the good son-in-law.

4. *Friends:* Seems like a different person. Kind, fair, respects their fundamental worth and their basic liberties. Loyal. Can get angry without blowing up.

5. *Job:* An assistant manager at a sporting goods store. Seen as responsible by boss. Generally fair with coworkers and customers, but can be rigid, defensive. Loyal. Some problems respecting and following authority but never major.

6. *Community:* Essentially ignores community issues unless they affect him directly. Not particularly responsible or giving. Has had several unnecessary confrontations with Asian-American neighbors. Problems with respect for authority when confronted by the police. Was almost arrested after a shouting match with an officer.

7. *Country:* Very little involvement other than complaining. Votes intermittently. Has superficial knowledge of current events. Shuts out other opinions. Not responsible or fair for the most part but does try to obey laws. Loyal to country. Is outraged when people are

treated unfairly by the system. Stresses individual rights and liberty.

8. *Society in General:* Is vocal against injustice. Condemns other countries with fewer liberties. Lacks respect for people whom he sees as markedly different on the basis of race, ethnicity, religion, or sexual orientation. Tends to think about and judge others in broad categories. Committed, responsible to the environment, recycles, tries not to waste.

As you can see, Eric's values are all over the place and often contradictory. So is his behavior. What he accepts on one level, he rejects or fails to practice on another. His friends think he's a considerate, fair guy. And they're right, he can be. But he can also be cruel, controlling, and bigoted. He is all of the above. While most of us do have variations and discrepancies in the way that we choose and apply values, Eric's pattern is particularly erratic and telling.

One look at this and you can see that he is very unhappy with himself, a factor that influences his interactions on all eight levels. But he's only marginally aware of his awful self-image. His sense of failure, inadequacy, and weakness doesn't really spring to the surface until it's triggered by his intimate relationship with his wife, Vanessa. He is terribly unhappy with this aspect of his life, but he needs Vanessa to survive emotionally.

As you might guess, he is happiest with his friends—as long as he has Vanessa to fall back on for emotional support. He appears to be fairly well balanced and moral in his treatment of friends. Likewise, he does well on the job, except for some predictable problems with authority and power. From that level on, he is only marginally involved. He is prejudiced, defensive, and close-minded about people and issues he doesn't understand. With a few exceptions, he is mostly preoccupied with himself and his immediate concerns.

The scope of Eric's moral world is extremely limited, stifling, and flat. He finds very little meaning or purpose in life and rarely escapes his self-made prison. You would expect him to be quite depressed. He is, in fact, but he doesn't really feel it until Vanessa temporarily withdraws her love. Eric has many psychological problems but he also needs to work toward a better balance in his moral life. That, in and of itself, can be a powerful, self-perpetuating way toward personal growth.

Vanessa's Values Profile

Vanessa's values are also out of whack, but the discrepancies tend to hurt her rather than other people. She actually has too much empathy and blames herself when things go wrong. Her own development is curtailed in the process. As you will see, she is repeating the patterns learned from her own parents. Her father, a police officer, was never physically abusive, but he seldom expressed positive emotions or showed other signs of approval. His style was to explode verbally at the slightest provocation, then make amends with gifts and special attention. Vanessa's mother worked to keep the peace. For Vanessa, as for her mother, "doing the right thing" means pleasing others and protecting their feelings.

1. *Self:* Very low self-esteem. No self-respect. Lies to herself. Treats herself unfairly, takes the blame. Ashamed and afraid of angry feelings—"I must be bad if I feel this way." Denies herself personal liberty by assuming submissive role with Eric.

2. *Intimate Relationships:* Treats Eric with caring, respect, and fairness but is dishonest. Lies for Eric by making up excuses. Lives to rescue Eric. In many ways, she becomes an "enabler." Because of this, her responsibility in the relationship is compromised. Extremely loyal to Eric—at the expense of other spheres in her life.

3. *Immediate and Extended Family:* Fails to act responsibly in protecting her son, who witnesses the physi-

cal and emotional abuse. Lies to her parents about the marriage. Ashamed that her marriage has turned out like theirs. Had been warned by her mother.

4. *Friends:* Vanessa is capable of deep friendships. Caring, respectful, responsible. Dishonest about her relationship with Eric. She is loyal to her friends, but loyalty to Eric comes first. Sees her friends less and less as Eric chips away at her liberty.

5. *Job:* Was a responsible worker—a dental hygienist. Has given up her job to raise their son, Eddie. Although she has intentions of going back, she could allow Eric to thwart those plans.

6. *Community:* Treats other well, follows all the basic values, but little if any involvement.

7. *Country:* Takes an active interest in national affairs, examines the many sides of complex issues. Votes regularly. Respects and follows just laws. Loyal.

8. *Society in General:* Considerate of different perspectives, cultures, and beliefs. Respects rights of others. Tries to live by the Golden Rule. Supports ideas of liberty and self-determination. Would like to be more involved in social causes but life currently centers on Eric and Eddie.

Vanessa's values are remarkably consistent when it comes to the treatment of other people, but she hardly applies them to herself. She appears to be her own worst enemy. Her major failures lie in level 1. She had vowed to avoid the submissive, self-defeating example set by her mother, but she is blind to her own emotional needs and patterns. Vanessa fails to see that she is duplicating her relationship with her father—fearing him, yearning for his approval, avoiding her own feelings, and living for the highs after the explosions. Her life is totally skewed, out of balance, and stifled by the cycle of abuse.

Aside from addressing the psychological issues, Vanessa

needs to expand her good values to the other levels of her life. Although overdone in her relationship with Eric, her empathy and caring are valuable assets that need other outlets. She needs to develop a renewed sense of responsibility toward herself and the community at large. She has the potential to enrich her life enormously.

Short Takes: Jennifer, David, and Shana

Let's take a look at the other players in our moral theater and see what's going on with their values.

Jennifer. Jennifer, you may remember, is the fifteen-year-old girl who became involved with an older male and his group of criminal friends. She has some vast discrepancies in her Values Profile, most of which are beyond her immediate awareness. Like Vanessa, Jennifer has low self-esteem and self-respect. With Scott, her twenty-year-old boyfriend, she is dependent, loyal, and approval-seeking. She treats him with caring and fairness but does not expect the same from him. She has little if any respect for her alcoholic mother but feels partly responsible for her welfare. She respects and cares for her grandmother, although she now lies to her constantly.

Jennifer's loyalty is almost exclusively reserved for her new friends, who are all involved in the same criminal activities. As part of their group, she plays fairly by their rules. But outside this circle, she violates standards of fairness, caring, respect, honesty, and responsibility. She has lost her sense of responsibility and respect for the larger community, as well as for the law.

Jennifer is heading for major trouble and an emotional breakdown. Her expected child will likely suffer at the hands of an erratic, inconsistent mother, just as Jennifer has. Given her immaturity and the serious discrepancies in her values, Jennifer is hardly prepared to raise a child. Even more troubling is her ability to shut down empathy at will. She is certainly capable of guilt, but this valuable emotion has been wiped out by boyfriend Scott's reassurances and the values he and his friends espouse. Shame and guilt will come back to haunt her.

David. David is the forty-seven-year-old corporate attorney having an extramarital affair with Shana, his twenty-seven-year-old legal assistant. (His story began on page 12). David is eating himself up with guilt. He dearly loves his wife, Noreen, but can't seem to let go of the exciting, almost addictive relationship with Shana. He holds himself to very high personal and moral standards across the social spectrum. He is well aware of his moral transgressions. In fact, he is a perfectionist who often has unrealistic expectations of himself and others. He is generally repressed, overcontrolled, and inhibited—as is his wife, Noreen. As he rediscovers emotional and physical fire with Shana, the values he holds on level 2 (intimate relationships) are taking a severe beating. He is juggling intimacy with two people simultaneously, while attempting to be loving, fair, respectful, honest, and loyal to each. Under the circumstances, this is impossible.

Furthermore, David is caught in a major ethical conflict at work. He is Shana's boss. Although he has not used this to manipulate her, the potential for abuse is implicit. David has no intention of ever misusing his power, but his judgment could easily be distorted in moments of anguish or passion. He cannot be an unbiased, fair boss—in spite of his best intentions. This lack of responsibility also puts his corporate employer in jeopardy. In a court of law, David could hardly prove his love or good intentions. These things are largely irrelevant in the decade of sexual harassment. Shana, in fact, has convinced herself that she is an innocent victim.

If David can get through all of this by breaking it off with Shana at all costs, he needs to allow himself to be a little more human, expressive, and spontaneous, and much less moralistic toward himself. Paradoxically, his unreasonable standards and overcontrol brought about what he feared most: humiliation, shame, and disgrace. He had been completely unprepared for the power of his feelings; like a flood, they literally swept him off his feet and threatened to wash away his life. There was no middle ground offering sanctuary.

Perhaps David will learn that he cannot always be the controlled, rational person he expects himself to be. There are stronger forces around that must be reckoned with, other sides of himself that must be developed. Even Richard, David's nineteen-year-old son, knew this when he said, "The guy needs to loosen up. Sometimes you just have to say 'screw it.'" Painfully prescient words indeed.

Shana.   Shana, David's twenty-seven-year-old mistress, turns moral flip-flops on all eight levels of social interaction. As you may remember, Shana had an ongoing sexual relationship in childhood with her stepfather, a long-distance truck driver who showered her with insincere praise and affection. The sexual relationship filled the void left by her depressed, preoccupied mother and made her feel alive and important. Shana's mother never saw her beautiful daughter as a separate person with needs and feelings of her own. Except for the selfish attention of her stepfather, Shana was very much alone, lost, and without a firm identity. For Shana, even though she had religious training and was taught values by her mother, doing the right thing meant doing anything that would take the pain away and fill the emptiness.

On the level of the self, Shana feels powerful, invincible, and morally superior one moment and worthless and empty the next. She is almost exclusively preoccupied with her own needs. She fears abandonment one moment, suffocation the next. She can be quite dishonest and subconsciously protects her self-image by lying.

Shana does not feel she can survive without an intimate relationship. To engage a potential partner, she lays a web of emotional tripwires around the partner's needs and vulnerabilities. This is not always a calculated move—she simply knows no other way. Love has to be captured with enticements and held in check with veiled threats. She is only superficially aware of the emotional needs of her partners; her magic lies in the sexual arena. She has a finely tuned, uncanny sense of her partner's physical needs and adapts herself accordingly. Sex gives her the illusion of power, wholeness, and fulfillment. Emotionally, she can be intensely loving and giving but only when her partner is meeting her seemingly endless needs. Most partners give up in sheer exhaustion.

When relationship problems inevitably occur, she blames her partner, minimizes responsibility, and firmly believes her distortions. Her loyalty is quite tenuous. Since Shana projects her own inadequacies on others, an idealized mate may suddenly become an object to vilify and hate. She soothes her own pain and sense of failure by seeking revenge. After the fall, her accounting of the events will be quite distorted. She will believe her own skewed perceptions.

Shana's friendships are superficial and almost always with males. Loyalty is a problem because she routinely breaks promises and confidences. She often lets people down. She tries to be fair, but most of the time she is highly judgmental and carries an overtly superior attitude. Respect gives way to rage when she feels hurt or slighted.

At work, Shana does relatively well for a short while because it's a structured situation and she knows what's expected. She's intelligent, articulate, attractive, and very engaging. However, her responsibility, loyalty, and honesty eventually break down as petty conflicts erupt with coworkers. At that point, she subconsciously plays people off against each other, sincerely believing her innocence all the while. This pattern was set years ago when relating to her stepfather and mother. Furthermore, she will violate rules and break laws if she has to, but is outraged when others do so. Outside of work, she is committed to several social causes involving animals and abused children.

Shana has serious personality problems that wreak havoc on her moral sense and the application of values. There is very little continuity or core to her personality. This is extremely frightening for her. She has devised all sorts of temporary ways to fill the void and quell the storms. Unfortunately, in her own mind, she falls back on childhood traumas to justify and excuse all of her transgressions. She is stuck in a self-perpetuating, self-defeating cycle.

FINDING THE RIGHT BALANCE

It's not likely that anyone can be perfectly consistent in applying the Incredible Seven values, between social levels or even on the same level. Nevertheless, it's extremely important to look at the particular values that you do stress and those that you may be ignoring. (To refresh your memory, here are the Incredible Seven: justice and fairness, caring, respect, responsibility, honesty, loyalty, and liberty).

If your values are moderately imbalanced, you might care a great deal about people but avoid making commitments to help them (*caring* is stressed, while *responsibility* is downplayed). You may stress *honesty* in all parts of your life but have very little toleration for people who might be different from you (a low level of *fairness* and *respect*). Or you might be so committed to the ideas of *justice, fairness,* and equality for a particular group of people that you'll downplay *honesty, caring,* and *respect* toward those who are not members of your cause.

Whenever these values get terribly out of balance, you'll feel it—one way or another—perhaps through guilt, shame, empty relationships, chronic interpersonal conflicts, or other gaping holes in the fabric of your life. It all boils down to that old adage, "What goes around, comes around." But sainthood isn't necessary. The key here is to periodically run a Values Profile on yourself. For all the trade-offs and compromises that you make, you should at the very least be aware of the other worthy values that you may be neglecting or overriding.

(Psychotherapists and other readers interested in the technical aspects of combining psychotherapy and values assessment might wish to consult *The Mystery of Goodness and the Positive Moral Consequences of Psychotherapy,* by Mary Nicholas, Ph.D., Norton, 1994. Dr. Nicholas' conceptual

framework and personal observations are particularly enlightening.)

THE BEST OF INTENTIONS

A while back, I mentioned that self-knowledge and doing the
right thing go hand in hand. I'm certain you know those pigheaded people who believe they're living by values such as
the Incredible Seven and are convinced that their perspective is clear, unbiased, and proper. If you happen to question
these myopic souls, they're likely to give a million reasons
to justify their actions. And there's simply too many of their
ilk in the world. It's time to fight back.

Well, we've met the enemy, and the enemy is us. We all
fall victim to our own psychological shenanigans. Try as we
might to be rational and objective, our emotional bugaboos,
personal biases, and self-serving thinking patterns often sabotage the best of intentions and provide fuel for the worst.
It's time to look at the psychological side of good people and
their bad deeds.

FIVE

Fooling Yourself:
Blind Spots and Other
Psychological Shenanigans

Doing the right thing and treating others with kindness and fairness may be an admirable goal, but life is never so simple. How many times have you intended to do the right thing, gotten sidetracked by more compelling personal needs, then convinced yourself that your actions "weren't really that bad"? How many times have you hurt yourself or others and made excuses to save face? How many times have you fooled yourself in love and done hurtful things you wouldn't ordinarily do? Or lied to avoid punishment? Cheated on your income taxes? You are, after all, a good person. Aren't you?

Since most of us, of course, are good people, who is creating all the havoc out there? Is the world dominated by psychopaths and moral degenerates? It may seem that way, but it's not likely. The world is dominated by people like us, people with an enormous capacity to unwittingly fool themselves and others by using a vast repertoire of mind games. This is the stuff of everyday life, the legerdemain of "normal" people.

Sometimes our mind games are adaptive and help us to hold reality at bay while we muster our resources. Sometimes we even lie and deceive out of concern and compassion for others. "You really are a great person and I'd love to go out with you, but I need some space right now." But at other times our psychological shenanigans are extremely detrimental and provide the fertile soil for our little demons,

84

bad deeds, and hurtful acts. What are these mind games, where do they come from, and how do they work? The first clue can be found by looking at the deepest part of ourselves.

PAINTING THE SELF-PORTRAIT

At the core of absolutely everything we think, feel, and do lies our *self-concept*. The self-concept is a living, growing, multidimensional *self-portrait* of who we *think* we are. It begins at birth and evolves layer by layer as we interact with significant people.

As we mature, our self-portrait changes, at least on the surface. A self-portrait in adolescence is likely to be quite different from that of an adult, yet the ghost image still resides within the adult portrait. Certain situations or things— a high school reunion, a picture, a fragrance, a song, or even a trauma such as rape—can, for better or worse, trigger the ghost images of a former portrait.

A self-portrait, then, is composed of overlapping, intermingling layers, some of which may even contradict each other. Knowing "who you are" can sometimes be quite confusing, particularly if old images are activated. Are you the controlled, competent, intelligent adult known to your colleagues at work, the irreverent comedian known to your best friends, or the uncertain, sensitive child who lives in your parents' memories? Probably all of the above. Somehow we manage to incorporate many different features into our self-portrait, emphasizing the qualities that we like, while hiding the ones that make us cringe. But in spite of all the ghost images and various features that make up a self-concept or picture of ourselves, most of us harbor a very basic assumption that remains fairly consistent throughout life:

"I'm Basically a Good Person"

Sound familiar? I've heard this line from people who have murdered, raped, abused, robbed, and grossly violated others. I've said it to myself after slipping into murky waters. Nearly everyone subscribes to this belief, regardless of the values he or she holds. Unless you're seriously depressed, you probably do also. You may dislike certain aspects or shortcomings about yourself and the bad things you've done, but underneath it all you need to believe that you're basically good. *In fact, your self-portrait is drawn around this extremely important assumption.* Your emotional survival may depend upon it.

Where does this assumption come from? If we're loved consistently as children, we're likely to have a very strong sense that we are good. This sense of goodness dominates our self-portrait until we do something bad, and badness, for most people, triggers all sorts of anxiety, shame, and guilt. Being good feels good. Being bad feels bad. Being bad is a direct threat to our ideas of personal goodness.

So unless we're depressed, under extreme stress, or habitually self-denigrating, our self-portrait is painted in a way that emphasizes the good person we believe ourselves to be. In fact, we work so hard to preserve the self-portrait that we're likely to ward off or ignore information that might threaten its basic integrity. Thus begins a great juggling act, born of the need for emotional protection.

THE SECURITY PATROL: GATEKEEPERS

The self-portrait is crucial for personal survival since it forms the basis of our relationship with the world. Like a priceless portrait hanging in the grand hall of a castle, it must be protected against harm. So what happens when intruders threaten the image of "good person"? Every castle, of course, has gatekeepers and a security patrol. And so do we.

The job of the gatekeepers (also known as "schemas" in the parlance of cognitive psychology) is to examine and organize every piece of information going in and out of our psychological castle. Information that contradicts or threatens our self-portrait is either filtered out, diluted, held hostage in one of several memory rooms or, if those methods don't work, twisted ever so slightly to temper the threat. It's a lot easier and quicker for the gatekeepers to color perceptions than to set off a major upheaval in the self.

In addition, the gatekeepers have a direct, two-way connection to our long-term memory banks. They make split-second decisions concerning what is relevant to the self and what is not. In fact, the gatekeepers and our long-term memory work in tandem to determine what information will be admitted to memory, what it means, and the form it might take when recalled, if at all. The gatekeepers, then, are guided by memory and the things that we have learned from experience. Memory, in turn, relies on the gatekeepers to quickly screen out information that doesn't seem pertinent. A nice arrangement.

Under Cover

The most important thing to know about the gatekeepers is this: They work automatically, that is, subliminally, behind the scenes, nanoseconds before anything is allowed to enter our immediate awareness, through either our senses or our memory banks. This means that all of our perceptions and memories have been filtered and *biased in* varying degrees by the time they register in our conscious mind. We never truly know what or how much has been filtered, shunted off to some obscure memory bank, or distorted by the gatekeepers. All we know is the information that gets through. Or we know nothing at all.

Our gatekeepers, then, have the enormous power to shape the way we view and respond to reality. In their efforts to screen, sort, and protect, they act as spin doctors, transforming information while searching for compromises that will appease the self, without unduly testing the gullibility of other people. While this activity may be necessary for survival in a complex, threatening world, it doesn't come without cost: self-deception.

THE TWISTS AND TURNS
OF SELF-DECEPTION

Self-deception is the price we pay for skewing reality. Sometimes it serves as a minor, helpful analgesic: "He rejected me because he's not ready for a relationship." Other times it gets totally out of hand and compromises our ability to deal effectively with the world: "He doesn't mean what he's saying. I know he really loves me." As the gatekeepers chip away at reality and select what enters consciousness, self-deception pops up in several different forms:

- self-serving, biased interpretations of events,
- a selective focus that leads to blind spots,
- a skewed reasoning process that allows us to see what we expect to see and believe what we need to believe, and
- a multitude of excuses for our actions, before and after they occur.

When exaggerated, all of these twists and turns interfere with our potential to do the right thing. (We'll see how this actually works later.)

Before going on, a word about *lying*. Many of the distortions described above generally transpire *without* our full awareness. Deliberate lying is another matter. When we lie, it's usually under our conscious control. The gatekeepers process the information without much ado since we're probably aware that we're lying to avoid disapproval, spare someone's feelings, avoid punishment, or lessen personal responsibility. Lying runs the gamut from little white lies— "that book you wrote was absolutely great"—to destructive whoppers that wipe out trust and respect or even kill people. For better or worse, deliberate lying is an undeniable, even necessary part of our daily existence. Situations can and do override the general moral imperative for honesty.

The moral dilemmas and trade-offs in those situations can be daunting.

Self-deception, on the other hand, implies that our gate-keepers have tidied things up in the psychological castle and given us a partially edited version of reality. We may not be fully aware that the end product has been edited. As you have seen, this puts us at great risk of creating overly protective, positive illusions about ourselves and deceiving or misleading others because of our own self-deception. The upshot is that we can unwittingly become entangled in things that contradict our basic values.

According to the extensive research of R. F. Baumeister at Case Western Reserve University in Ohio, C. R. Snyder at the University of Kansas, and other prominent cognitive psychologists, our psychological gatekeepers have some fascinating and overzealous tricks at their disposal. Let's take a closer look at these as they apply in everyday life.

THE THINGS I TELL MYSELF

You're smarter than average, fairly good looking, and generally more reasonable, responsible, and perceptive than most people. That's my opinion (since you're reading my book), and probably your opinion as well. And when you're successful in any endeavor, it's probably because you work hard and have some admirable talents. Right? When you're given praise, it probably feels well deserved and right on target, in spite of your humble soft-shoe. You've had your share of bad luck, but you've persevered. Furthermore, your dog or cat is exceptionally bright and has some remarkable, even uncanny abilities. Not one to jump to conclusions, you've found plenty of evidence to confirm these observations. And, of course, you're a damned good person, even though you screw up at times.

Absolutely. I won't question it for a moment. In fact, it's true of me, too. But why do most of us feel this way? And why is it the other person who's just "average" or generally lacking? The guy down the street looks like a dork, drives like a maniac, supports outrageous political agendas, ignores his lawn, blathers inanities, and struts around like Rambo. You don't like him and he deserves it. Never mind that he's the chief of police. Furthermore, his dog wets on your bougainvillea.

Shades of Gray and the Self-Serving Bias

About the only thing that isn't open to interpretation and debate in the last two paragraphs is the fact that your hypothetical neighbor's dog commits indiscretions on your plants. Everything else involves opinion, interpretation, and shades of gray. The observations could, in fact, be quite accurate, but without better evidence, it's difficult to be certain. In so much of life, conclusive evidence is not available.

The point here is that most of us with an adequate dose of self-esteem see *ourselves* through tinted glasses, while reserving our more skeptical eye for others. Even if you're extremely self-critical, you have a basic survival mechanism, a *self-serving bias* that tries to give each shade of gray a positive, self-confirming spin. If your self-esteem is very low, the unconscious spin could go either way: negative, to confirm your inadequate image; or positive, to avoid hurting it any further. The latter is more probable.

In any case, the gatekeepers, like certain politicians, have a ball with anything slightly gray that's open to interpretation. For instance, while you can hardly deny that you failed an exam, you and your gatekeepers can easily skew the reasons why: The test was unfair, you were ill or depressed, it was a bad hair day, and so forth. And unless you get overwhelming feedback from other people contesting your reasons, you're likely to accept them. And if a sympathetic friend colludes with your reasons, you're home free. At least in your mind.

Looking again at the generic "you" described above, we

can see all sorts of ways that the self-serving bias creeps in. For one thing, "you," no offense intended, are likely to attribute your successes at work to your admirable talents and smarts, while at the same time downplaying your failures. If you do acknowledge failure, it could be softened or blamed on a number of debatable things such as an unfair boss, lousy working conditions, sexism, racism, bad luck, or overwhelming family problems. Maybe these things are true. The point is, *you're apt to accept the successes without question* but go through all sorts of mental gyrations to soften the failures. In reality, perhaps you're successful because your cousin owns the business.

In the same manner, the positive evaluations you receive at work and elsewhere are, of course, extremely accurate and well deserved. The negative comments, you believe, may have a grain of truth but could be overblown due to a misunderstanding, an unfortunate, isolated incident, or your boss's unreasonable expectations. Thank God. There's room here to squirm and save face.

Whether you truly accept the feedback as it stands depends upon your trust in the evaluator, how closely it jibes with other evidence, your emotional stability, and your willingness to modify your self-portrait. That can be a tall order. It's easier to zero in on and accept those things that confirm the good. Thus, you can build and maintain a positive self-portrait in spite of your failings and hurtful behaviors. And chances are, you are better than your neighbor.

Seeing and Not Seeing

Our psychological gatekeepers have the capacity to act as a zoom lens, focusing sharply on pertinent matters while leaving an impressionistic, soft background. All sorts of things may be going on around you while you're reading an engrossing book, but for the most part, you shut them out or pay little attention. You don't want to be disturbed. A plant may be drooping and in need of water, the cat clawing the rug, your lower back aching, or your neighbor bellowing at his wife. You are aware of these things on some level since you know where *not* to look. The gatekeepers filter the input and divert your attention to the book. You see but you don't see. Some of the filtered information—the potentially annoying or upsetting stuff—may go directly to memory without your conscious awareness.

The same process holds true for emotional things that could have an impact on our self-portrait, the image of people and things we care about, and our personal beliefs. We all have *blind spots,* defensive gaps, and areas of diminished focus ... like the ratty but comfortable chair in the living room that we don't truly notice until company comes. Like the lump in a breast. Like our insensitive, hurtful behavior. Like horrendous events elsewhere that don't immediately affect our lives.

Anyone who has been jilted in love knows, without a doubt, how blind spots can happen. Overwhelmed by joy, hope, great expectations, and chemistry, it's all too easy to disregard or minimize the warning signs. To put them into focus would mean to acknowledge the possibility that we're wasting our time, that we're giving our heart and soul to a person who doesn't really want us, that we're probably making a fool of ourselves, and that we're about to suffer a humiliating loss. We have perfectly good reasons for not seeing. (For a fascinating look at self-deception and love, see *Breaking Hearts: The Two Sides of Unrequited Love,* by R. F. Baumeister and S. Wotman, published by Guilford Press in 1992.)

In the extramarital affair with his twenty-seven-year-old legal assistant, Shana, David is so taken with her drama, risk-taking, and passion that he soft-peddles her more disturbing, manipulative qualities. As he said earlier, losing her would "be like killing off an exciting new part of myself." David does see, but most of it is out of focus. He's setting himself up for a devastating lawsuit, as well as a shattered relationship with his family.

Shana can be very difficult at times, but like me, she's under a lot of stress. Although she tends to be temperamental, demanding, and unpredictable, it's all part of the wild spirit that I value in her. Like anything, it's a trade-off. I know she hurts a lot inside— things from her childhood—so it's no wonder that this spills over into our relationship from time to time. It's a miracle that she's able to love me as she does. I sometimes wonder what she's done with all the hurt and resentment that's been a part of her life.

Noreen, David's wife of twenty years and a public relations consultant, also sees without seeing. To see would trigger unbearable thoughts about the future and her own sense of adequacy. She has invested so heavily in David, his decency, and their relationship that his betrayal is unthinkable.

He's been coming home later and later. I keep telling him he's working too hard. He looks so drawn and exhausted. Sometimes I think he's staying at work to avoid coming home—all the responsibilities, tasks, and humdrums. I'm tired of it all, too. I wish we could just go away together, have some time for ourselves, rekindle things. He's just so preoccupied. I know he means well. I'll do my best to help him through this midlife crisis.

Believing What You Need to Believe

Suppose your car won't start in the rain and you're terribly late for work. You run to the nearest bus stop and wait impatiently for the bus that never seems to come. Finally, off in the foggy distance behind the signs and buried in the glare of oncoming traffic, you make out the shape of a large red and white vehicle. Your reasoning kicks in. "It's probably the bus. Buses here are big, red, and white." A boy runs to the curb and digs in his pocket, perhaps for some money. "It must be the bus. About time!" You step off the curb like an idiot as the red and white cement mixer belches diesel fumes and splashes muck over your shoes.

Our mental gatekeepers, those cognitive guardians that examine, identify, and organize everything going in and out of our brains, have an obnoxious way of fooling us like that. The thing is, they have to filter through and categorize input from all the senses very quickly, often without all the evidence at their disposal. In the above example they're primed to see a bus. To do this, they focus selectively as described earlier and refer to a "bus" template stored in our memory. If what they're seeing matches the template in some way—say, shape and size—they'll probably look for another attribute, such as color, to confirm the sighting.

If the color matches, it's very likely that the gatekeepers will tentatively stick the sighting in the "bus" category. When the boy runs out to the curb, it's a done deal. They've found what they were looking for and shut out additional information; never mind the humongous cylindrical thing churning on top or the fact that the boy simply spotted a friend. Getting the sighting into the "bus" category can be quick and easy; getting it out is another matter entirely. Dripping anger, you might even swear you were splashed by a bus.

The same holds true for many of our more abstract beliefs. Try as we might to be fair and objective, our needs and expectations unwittingly bias our reasoning process. In essence, we need a bus, we look for evidence that *confirms* rather than *refutes* a bus—and we get run over by a cement mixer. *We engage our selective focus to look for the things we want to see and use that information as logical evidence for our desired conclusion.*

Magicians work wonders with this principle. So do some politicians, certain talk show hosts, cult leaders, and demagogues. In fact, this kind of biased reasoning happens all the time, even in the sciences where exacting measurements are possible. Unfortunately, we're all prone to biased reasoning, particularly when we're trying to make sense of shades of gray, resolve moral dilemmas, and do the right thing.

FOOLING OURSELVES AND OTHERS
WITH EXCUSES

This is the situation so far: Your self-portrait (self-concept) is based on certain assumptions about yourself, one of them being that you're basically a good person. The portrait hangs in the great hall of your psychological castle and is protected by a security patrol. The security patrol is composed of gate-keepers (schemas) who work behind the scenes to sort through all information before it reaches the self-portrait. Information that seriously challenges the portrait is screened out, diluted, or reconstructed.

As helpful as this activity may be, it sets up a self-serving bias, which thrives on shades of gray. The bias can lead to blind spots and faulty or incomplete reasoning, which in turn can lead to good people doing bad things. To varying degrees, we all fall prey to such self-deception, even though we might swear otherwise. That's the nature of the game.

Now, what happens when other people get involved? It would be a relatively easy matter to keep fooling ourselves without any serious checks on reality. But we can only go so far in our self-deception before it collides head-on with the skeptical eye of other people or our own conscience. Conscience, you may remember, develops through the approval and disapproval of our parents and other important people.

In anticipation of such a challenge, we're likely to back down a bit, flounder around in those shades of gray, and come up with "reasons" for what we've done or are about to do. We may be aware that we're looking for reasons but largely unaware how much they've been pushed and pulled by the self-protective gatekeepers. The reconstituted "reasons," of course, usually take the form of *excuses.*

Psychologists have been studying the nature of excuses for years. At the forefront has been the extensive research of C. R. Snyder at the University of Kansas. (Much of the earlier research in excuse-making is presented in *Excuses: Masquerades in Search of Grace,* by C. R. Snyder, R. Higgins, and R. Stucky, published in 1983 by Wiley-Interscience.) Since then, Snyder and other colleagues have worked to identify what triggers our excuses, the form they take, and how they regulate our perceptions of personal responsibility. We'll look at a typical array of excuses later. First, let's see where they come from and how they work.

"It's Not an Excuse, It's a Fact!"

Or so it seems. Because of our built-in bias system, it's often very difficult to know how far off base we may be. (Sometimes we do know but persist anyhow.) But one thing is clear: Our defenses are immediately and automatically engaged whenever anyone asks that nerve-wracking question, *"Why did you do that?"* By the time we reach adolescence, we're experts at tailoring excuses to that and similar questions. Through experience, we've learned that some answers are more acceptable than others.

If an important person such as a parent, spouse, or close friend believes our explanation or tells us what we want to hear, it gains the status of *social reality.* No longer just existing in your mind, the excuse has the look and feel of a fact. We'll probably defend it to the end, particularly if it incorporates several grains of truth. Even if others don't totally buy the excuse, the simple act of putting the excuse into words makes it seem more real and valid, at least from our viewpoint. On some level, we make a commitment to our excuse.

Getting Too Close: Haggling Over Responsibility

How do our psychological gatekeepers size up something and "decide" that an excuse is necessary? What triggers their decision to taint the truth? According to Snyder's research, our self-serving gatekeepers ask two major questions about any event that might affect us. The first is, *"How much am I to blame?"* As you might imagine, the answer is a "negotiated responsibility."

For example, if you turn around in a china shop and the end of your bag or briefcase sends dishes flying, the gatekeepers are likely to panic. *You klutz! How could you do such a thing? Do you realize what this will cost? And all these people are staring at you!* In the embarrassment of the moment, you'll probably apologize profusely and offer to pay the damages. There's little doubt in your mind that you *caused* the mishap, even if it was an accident. After all, your parents taught you to take responsibility for your actions.

On the other hand, depending upon your personality and the level of responsibility instilled by your parents, your gatekeepers may scurry to capitalize on those notorious shades of gray. In the few seconds that it takes the store clerk to arrive, your gatekeepers may size up the width of the aisle, the distance between displays, and the stability of similar china arrangements on the shelf. "Look, I'm sorry, but I couldn't help it. It was an accident waiting to happen. There's simply no room to move in this store. You're trying to push too much merchandise. You're lucky I didn't fall with the dishes!" With this maneuver, you save face and *distance* yourself from the *cause* of the event. Reality is transformed ever so slightly to get you off the hook. This kind of response could be habitual and automatic.

According to Snyder, our gatekeepers send us a biased appraisal regarding our level of tie-in with the cause of an event. If the event is positive, it's closely linked with the self: *"My* company outperformed everyone this year." As the balance sheet becomes increasingly negative, the gatekeepers strive to create a distance: "Last year *they* couldn't do anything right." Unless we're steeped in self-blame, we typically resort to all sorts of conscious and semiconscious excuses to distance ourselves from causes and negative events. So what? Everybody does it!

Really, Now . . . It's Not That Bad

While the gatekeepers are negotiating our level of responsibility surrounding an event, they're also asking a second major question, *"How bad is it?"* As the event dips toward the "bad" end of the good-bad scale (according to our personal judgment), our excuse-making mechanism is placed on ready alert. The gatekeepers are fully prepared to take the "bad" edge off the event and give it a more positive spin, even if they don't necessarily deny responsibility: "I only broke two small dishes, it's not so bad," "I only hit her a couple of times. She deserved it. There weren't even any bruises," or "I cheated on the exam because the professor is impossible." The tactic is to minimize the extent of the "badness," offer justifications, or criticize another person.

MY EXCUSES, YOUR EXCUSES

As you have seen, the biased answers to the two major questions *"How much am I to blame?"* and *"How bad is it?"* will shape the form of our excuses. If we're closer to the cause of the event than we'd like to believe, we'll shape our excuses to reduce our connection. If our actions stray into the "bad" domain, we'll make excuses that shift them away from that end of the spectrum. It's "perfectly reasonable." And we all do it, at least initially. With further reflection, we may reprimand the gatekeepers and request another assessment. This, of course, depends upon our degree of self-knowledge, emotional stability, and character.

Here's a table of some common excuses and tactics identified by Snyder and other cognitive psychologists. Variations abound, and some may be closer to the truth than others. Nevertheless, initiating or hearing any of these basic forms should set off a few alarms. We, or the other person, could be heading for self-deception. How far is the excuse from the truth? You decide.

BENCHMARK NO. 4

THE TOP TEN EXCUSES: FOOLING YOURSELF

EXCUSES	TACTICS
1. *"I didn't do it."*	Outright denial, a lie—in spite of evidence.
2. *"He made me do it."*	Blaming others.
3. *"I did it but I had no choice."*	Claiming mitigating circumstances.
4 *"I really didn't mean to."*	Becomes an excuse if used time and again to deny hurtful intentions.
5. *"I don't know what came over me—I just lost control."*	The behavior is alien, not really a part of the good person within.
6. *"It really wasn't that bad; I only did it a little."*	Minimizing the consequences and implications of the act.
7. *"I did it for your own good."*	Justifying.
8. *"It's over and done with. It has nothing to do with today. Let's forget about it."*	Isolating the event in the past, as if it has no impact on the present and future.
9. *"He's such a jerk. He deserved it anyhow."*	Degrading the other person to lessen the implications of the act.

10. *"Everybody does it."* If others behave in the same manner, it can't be so bad.

Excuse-making isn't the only process going on behind the scenes. In the next chapter, we'll look a bit deeper and see how some other unconscious traps work to undermine our better judgment.

SIX

Beyond Your Awareness:
Unconscious Traps
and Bad Deeds

As you have seen, excuses protect us by acting as cover stories, diminishing our level of responsibility and sanitizing our behavior. Most of the time, we have some degree of awareness, however faint, that we're searching for reasons and rationalizations. We just happen to believe them. But that's not the whole story. There's another, fascinating realm of self-deception taking place exclusively on the unconscious level. It is here that many good people lose their way.

DEFENSIVE TRICKS

Several years ago, I ran into a childhood friend whom I hadn't seen for a long while. As we reminisced, we talked about our mutual fear of public speaking. He joked about a humiliating incident in an early elementary class that we both attended:

> I'll never forget it. Each child had to stand in front and talk about his summer vacation. As you know, I was timid and shy, so I waited for my turn in absolute terror. By the time I got up there, I just froze and stared at the kids, eventually stammering and making little sense. They laughed at me. God, I'll never forget their faces. Total embarrassment. But somehow I continued and got through. They applauded.

I was stunned by his recollection. In my mind, the memory was clear as day: He did freeze and stammer, but that's not all. He wet his pants, a noticeable dribble the size of a half dollar, and ran from the room in total humiliation and shame. He didn't return for two days. His classmates, having been given a stern lecture by the teacher, seldom brought up the incident again. In fact, they were remarkably supportive.

What gives here? Naturally, I kept my mouth shut but couldn't help wondering whose memory was in error. Since the event wasn't a trauma for me, I suspected that his rendition was doctored by the psychological gatekeepers. My suspicions were eventually confirmed. Unfortunately, the quizzical look on my face triggered some uncomfortable snippets of forgotten memory for my friend. He looked pained but said nothing.

In our next meeting, he asked for my memory of his talk. With great reluctance, I recounted how he had bolted out of the room. He supplied the humiliating details. His shame rose to the surface with all the force of the original, but it was disarmed by good humor and honesty.

We shared a few more childhood humiliations. He brought up some events involving me, which I did remember—down to particular details—but I hadn't remembered my emotional reactions. In those cases, my memory was that of the detached observer, or so it seemed. With others, I had forgotten almost all the details but was grossly aware of the feelings, which were still alive and kicking. Other events were forgotten altogether. I had forgotten that I had forgotten. The same was true for my friend.

Damage Control

My friend and I both felt we were recounting the truth. We had no intention of deceiving each other. Our renditions were as accurate as our memories allowed. Therein lies the rub. Somehow things had gotten twisted going into memory or coming out. And had we not run into each other, chances are we would have retained our illusions and blissful ignorance. Truth has a price.

Our psychological gatekeepers can be very resourceful when faced with painful trauma, overwhelming feelings, taboo thoughts, shame, and guilt. As you saw in chapter 5, the gatekeepers are the mental security guards, the cognitive schemas that interact with, organize, and sometimes even shape the signals coming from our senses. One of their functions is to protect our self-image and emotional well-being. They are masters at regulating, biasing, and deflecting the flow of information going into and out of our memory banks and awareness. They shape our initial perception of an event for better or worse but they also attempt some damage control later on. The extent of their work depends upon our personality and emotional strength. Some people require very little damage control, while others operate on a hair trigger, engaging defenses at the slightest provocation. But we all need some degree of emotional protection.

Shaping What Goes Into Memory

As the gatekeepers work, certain aspects of the event are diverted through a maze of interconnecting, convoluted pathways, where they are shaped on their way to the memory banks. Other aspects get through relatively unscathed. A smell, a touch, or a certain look may be burned into memory, while the memory of a conversation might be modified to include things you wanted to say but didn't.

Sometimes the gatekeepers respond to our fears and expectations and skew incoming memories for the worse. The event is exaggerated and overblown with or without damage control. That snarling monster of your childhood may have been a miniature schnauzer. Our memory banks, then, are fed information that has been biased either way by the gatekeepers, as well as more accurate perceptions of the event. As you saw in chapter 5, *our emotional needs, expectations, and vulnerabilities determine what gets skewed, in what direction, and how much.*

Controlling What Comes Out

The gatekeepers do more than shape memory input. They must also control the information that's released from memory. In addition to sorting and processing this information, they also *repress* or block certain memories or parts of memories from recall and awareness. Unless threads of the repressed memory slip out, we're hardly aware that we're missing anything. Thus, when we attempt to recall an emotional event from the immediate or distant past, parts of it might be held hostage in memory and parts of it might be released as is, while other aspects could be doctored by a variety of defensive tricks.

The "defensive tricks" I'm referring to here are, of course, the unconscious "defense mechanisms" often addressed in psychotherapy or psychoanalysis. Although they take many forms (denial, isolation, projection, splitting, regression, and so forth), the defense mechanisms are all based on some degree of repression, which holds certain thoughts and feelings at bay.

For example, you may deny saying something hurtful, "forget" important dates, attribute your own unacceptable feelings to someone else, split people and events into black-and-white categories, transfer anger toward one person to someone else, and so on—all without your awareness.

My friend *repressed* the fact that he had wet his pants and replaced it with something more acceptable, applause and acceptance. In another recalled memory, he *denied* that he had had a mad infatuation with a certain girl who rejected him. I knew differently. In my own case, I remembered certain events but not my feelings. My friend insisted that I was extremely upset. I *isolated* myself from the pain or numbed myself to it. In still others, he needed to remind me of the factual details surrounding some still painful memories.

Trade-Offs

Defense mechanisms are extremely important for our emotional well-being, just as our immune system protects our physical survival. They reduce stress, keep certain feelings and impulses in check, and ward off emotional pain. We all use defense mechanisms to varying degrees because they work, at least for a while. But sometimes they get out of hand. When reality is tainted and skewed too much or too often, we pay a price in the form of additional psychic turmoil, interpersonal conflict, and poor judgment. We're doomed to repeat our mistakes, caught in a circular process that's beyond our awareness.

Habitually shutting out shame, guilt, anxiety, and other worrisome things about ourselves can lead to a sense of emptiness, chronic dissatisfaction, and a wide variety of psychological problems. Living in a defensive cocoon, we never really experience the liberating power of change and forgiveness.

Furthermore, the information we're trying to avoid, twist, or disguise can unwittingly seep into other areas of our lives, clouding judgment and subverting our attempts to do the right thing. *We're very likely to hurt others when we overprotect ourselves.* Thus, our defense mechanisms can seriously affect our moral life.

To see how this can happen, let's look at a very basic but powerful defense mechanism that, like repression, has the potential to routinely skew our moral vision. We'll look at some other defenses later.

SPLITTING: GOOD GUY, BAD GUY

Shana, the twenty-seven-year-old legal assistant having an affair with David, her married boss, has some serious personality problems that undermine her moral vision. As a child, she was involved in an incestuous relationship with her stepfather and was treated like a plastic doll by her depressed, self-centered mother. To handle the emptiness, inconsistency, and confusion, she unconsciously built her entire life around a powerful defensive trap called *splitting.* Although beyond her awareness, it has undermined her emotional stability, seriously disrupted her relationships, and grossly compromised her moral integrity.

Shana has immense difficulty seeing and handling shades of gray—a hallmark of the splitting process. In her mind, at any particular moment, people or ideas are either all good or all bad. When David meets her needs, he is idealized as a saint. When he fails in some regard or shows a negative emotion, he is suddenly demoted to the all-bad category. Her "love" can change to destructive hate on a moment's notice. She turns on people like a snake and is convinced that her actions are justified.

While Shana splits the external world into good and bad categories, she also does the same within herself. At different moments, according to the intensity and nature of the stress, Shana "splits off" the good, acceptable things about herself, while disowning the negative. Or sometimes the reverse happens and she falls into a deep despair.

What it boils down to is this: She simply does not have the emotional capacity to join contradictory feelings and impulses into a complete whole. When she feels "good," she is powerful and superior; when she feels "bad," she is the scum of the earth. Each feeling is experienced with great intensity, but at different moments, apart from the other. In a similar manner, certain needs, such as her need for closeness and security, cannot be reconciled with her need for control and independence. She'll jump from one extreme to the other, unaware of what's really going on.

Because of the splitting process, Shana's capacity for *moral discrimination* is seriously compromised. When she feels "all bad" about herself or other people, she's likely to behave in an abusive manner. When she feels good and splits off the bad parts of herself, she runs the risk of unfairly *projecting* those negative feelings onto other people. For example, she might be absolutely convinced that an innocent person is deceitful and conniving. She will color observations and misinterpret actions without realizing that her own negative qualities are fueling the distortion. She will blame others unjustly and deny personal responsibility. At other times, she'll be unreasonably contrite and self-denigrating. As good and bad flip-flop, so do her moral convictions.

No One Is Immune

Shana's case is an extreme example of the destructive power of splitting. We can see it more clearly in her life since it's so pronounced. But we *all* split to varying degrees, particularly when under stress. Think of the last time you were *really* angry at someone you cared about. At that particular moment, it's doubtful that you appreciated his or her better qualities. "You're a selfish, inconsiderate, unfeeling moron! Get out of my life!" In your hurt, you *devalued* the other person.

It's likely that the heat of the moment temporarily unraveled your capacity to see the whole person. Furthermore, the hurt you felt may have thrown blinders over your role in the conflict. It may have taken hours, days, or weeks for your vision to clear. Or perhaps you still can't see the other person's good qualities. You might deny ever feeling the affection you once felt.

In a similar manner, we all split off and deny parts of our inner selves, sometimes even the caring, compassionate parts. As a result, feelings such as shame, guilt, rage, hate, and fear can operate silently in the background, pulling our strings with great finesse, even as we claim otherwise. We may be quick to see and condemn these things in others. Righteous indignation feels better than insecurity.

Or, through splitting, we may see the world in good and bad stereotypes, lumping individuals of a particular race, nationality, profession, or other grouping into an impressionistic whole. In the extreme, as in the 1995 terrorist bombing of the federal building in Oklahoma City, destructive impulses are split off and given license for expression in simplistic black-and-white categories. "The federal government is an encroaching leech, sucking away our personal liberties. For our country's sake, like our revolutionary ancestors, we must use whatever means necessary to stop the oppression. The protection of freedom involves many sacrifices." Abhorrent, evil acts such as those committed in Oklahoma germinate and thrive in the fertile soils of the splitting process. Humane feelings are replaced by rhetoric and dogmatic "ideals," even if there is no evil, malicious intent. You'll see how splitting happens in groups in the next chapter.

Where Does Splitting Come From?

Splitting begins in infancy and forms the basis of a child's ability to discriminate between good and bad. In the infant's undeveloped mind, things are divided up according to how they feel. They're either good or bad. As the child matures, with help from his caregivers, he slowly gains the cognitive capacity to integrate conflicting feelings about himself and other people: "I broke the lamp but I'm still a good boy" or "Daddy is ignoring me now but he's the best."

The well-developed child, like most adults, will resort to some splitting when under stress. ("I hate you! You never let me do anything! At least Mom cares.") Nevertheless, to varying degrees, he has the capacity to still love Dad while he sorts through conflicting feelings.

How does it go wrong? Again, Shana's case is a good example. Her mother, you may remember, was depressed, self-involved, and oblivious to the family incest. She seldom showed love and approval unless Shana conformed exactly to her expectations. Shana's feelings were ignored or discounted. Rules were made and enforced arbitrarily, according to her mother's needs. Shana never knew what to expect and seldom felt safe and loved. When she was "bad," she was never given the opportunity to make amends or receive forgiveness. And, most certainly, her mother never sincerely apologized to her. Thus, Shana slowly began to disown negative aspects of herself, while at the same time trying to please and identify with the adult she depended upon.

This was a no-win situation. Shana needed to see her mother as "good" even though, down deep, Shana hated her. But to feel safe and secure, Shana had to idealize her mother by putting her on a pedestal and shutting out her shortcomings. The splitting process was taking shape.

The splitting became worse when Shana's stepfather began paying special attention to her. The shame of the sexual abuse was easily pushed aside by the tremendous feelings of power and security she now possessed. Her rage toward her mother surfaced while the stepfather became the "good" parent. She quickly learned to play him off against the "bad" mother.

In essence, Shana's environment was so inconsistent, unloving, insincere, and manipulative that she never understood that she could make mistakes and still be a kind, loving person. She never learned that it was natural and okay to love and hate someone at the same time. For her, it was total confusion, bouncing from one extreme to another. *As in infancy, good and bad were reduced to primitive feelings related to security and immediate gratification.* Unfortunately, we all fall into this trap to varying degrees.

OTHER DEFENSES, OTHER STORIES

David. David, the married attorney consumed and tormented by the tempestuous affair with Shana, is also caught in several unconscious traps. The traps were set in place long before his affair, and now, once engaged, threaten to pull him in even further. Many of David's vulnerabilities, past and present, stem from lack of self-awareness and *repressed* needs. He has driven himself to be a "moral," hardworking, successful person without truly acknowledging the "shadow" side of his personality. A perfectionist by nature, he has overcontrolled his more spontaneous, harmless impulses, and operated under the illusion that he could always control anything worse.

The problem is, he *denied* the extent of his sexual needs, his need for adventure and risk, and his need for change. This left him extremely vulnerable. Shana's attributes resonated with these unacknowledged needs and triggered a tidal wave. The feelings were so intense that David lost his way. In his own mind, he *rationalized* what was going on. "It's wrong, but this must happen to everyone sooner or later. I'll see to it that no one will get hurt. My wife will never know and Shana never stays with anyone long enough to get hurt."

He even began to unjustly blame his unhappiness on his wife, Noreen. He saw her as repressed, driven by security, and sexually inhibited. Some of this was true but the extent of his assessment was distorted by *projection.* He was rejecting the suffocating aspects of himself and seeing them as emanating from Noreen. Free of her for extended moments with Shana, he was now free from himself, or so it seemed. The immense pain of his moral prison quickly dispelled that notion.

Eric. Eric is the twenty-six-year-old assistant sporting goods manager who emotionally browbeats and physically abuses Vanessa, his wife. He blames Vanessa for his lack of control and hides his own sense of inadequacy under a cloak of bravado. He must always be in charge. Unfortunately, he has little, if any, control over the unconscious forces that bandy him about and fuel his immoral behavior.

As you may remember, Eric was raised in an authoritarian atmosphere that deteriorated into harsh, arbitrary physical punishment. His father was physically abusive and emotionally cruel to Eric and the entire family. Although Eric's mother was generally overindulgent in her parenting style, his father's authoritarian style dominated. While Eric was fearful and resentful of his father, he unconsciously defended himself by *identifying with his aggressor.* If he could become strong and invincible like his father, perhaps he could win his approval and avoid mistreatment.

To identify with his father, Eric had to demean and disown certain things about his mother and himself. The caring and compassion he felt coming from his mother were vital for his emotional well-being, but he overtly dismissed these feelings as weak and "feminine." He *rationalized* that she deserved what she got because she was inadequate and naive. Like his father, Eric blocked out a great deal of empathy for his mother. And when he was abused, his own shame and humiliation were *split off* and *repressed.* Even today, he remembers many of the beatings and the physical pain but the associated feelings have been lost.

Since there was no natural flow of give-and-take or freedom of discussion in Eric's family, he quickly learned that there were good guys and bad guys, winners and losers. Like Shana, but to a lesser extent, he had trouble seeing two sides of an issue at the same time. To avoid the anxiety of ambiguity, he learned to dig in and hold his ground. His views mimicked his father's and were based on a need for security and control rather than on careful reasoning. Doing the right thing meant stemming the chaos and resolving conflicts with force.

Today, he *projects* his own shame, fear, and sense of inadequacy on Vanessa and believes that these shortcomings are emanating from her. He needs Vanessa but holds her in great contempt. In fact, he relates to the world in this manner, *displacing* or redirecting much of his rage toward people he does not value. Most of what is bad lies "out there" rather than within. He's quick to hurt, fight, or destroy the "bad," while ignoring his own demons. Eric's gatekeepers are working overtime.

Vanessa. Eric's twenty-four-year-old abused wife is steeped in *denial* of his behavior and her own role in perpetuating it. She makes excuses for her husband and assumes the blame when things go wrong. She fails to confront Eric and minimizes the effect of the fighting on Eddie, their two-year-old son.

As you saw in chapter 4, Vanessa does have many strengths and positive attributes. Her values of fairness, caring, and respect are remarkably consistent and admirable when it comes to the treatment of other people, but she hardly applies them to herself. Unfortunately, she is blind to her own *repressed* emotional needs and to the dynamics that keep her entangled in a "codependent" relationship. She fails to see that much of her own rage and hurt is expressed indirectly through Eric.

The source of this circular dynamic goes back to her own family, where she was made to feel guilty about anger. Her father, a police officer, was never physically abusive, but he seldom expressed positive emotions or showed other signs of approval. If Vanessa or her mother disagreed or expressed their own negative feelings, he would explode and berate them. Vanessa felt that her own needs didn't count. To avoid being "bad," she hid her feelings behind a compliant, loving façade. Only her father was allowed to express negative feelings.

For Vanessa, it was always safer to feel bad about herself. To keep the peace and win her father's approval, she followed her mother's lead and assumed responsibility and blame. Doing the right thing meant pleasing others and protecting their feelings. She never meant to marry someone like her father, but the trap of familiarity was more powerful than her self-awareness. Unconsciously, she continues to re-create what she knows best. She and her son are paying a heavy price.

Jennifer.   Jennifer is the pregnant fifteen-year-old girl who became involved in criminal activities with Scott, her twenty-year-old boyfriend. Before meeting Scott and his friends, Jennifer tried hard to treat people in the same manner that she liked to be treated. Breaking into homes, stealing cars, and assaulting other people hardly seemed something she was capable of doing. But her turmoil and frustration were boiling beneath the surface, waiting for a catalyst such as Scott. And now, given apparent justification and full license for expression, her anger has been unconsciously *split off* and *displaced* on other people. She doesn't see it as originating within her self.

As a small child, Jennifer remembers *dissociating* while her mother drank. Her mother, you may remember, is a successful real estate agent who, lost in her own dependencies, gave Jennifer very little direction and consistent guidance. The only source of stability Jennifer had was her grandmother. Unfortunately, she was not always available. Jennifer devised her own ways of getting through her difficult childhood:

> Mom would start drinking and I knew, sooner or later, she'd get nasty and off the wall. There was nothing I could do so I'd sit on my bed, close my eyes, and pretend I was floating in a place between the moon and the stars. It was peaceful and I had no insides or body. Sometimes I could go there even when she'd put her nose in my face. I'd see her but I'd imagine that I was watching TV or something. If she got worse, I'd shout, "Mom, please stop it! Stop it! I love you!" She'd cry and hug me but it would all start again later. I hated her at those times. I'd just take my mind and go where I wanted.

When Jennifer steals from others or invades their homes, she partially dissociates by turning off her empathy and pretending that she is someone else—someone older, tougher, and more powerful. And now, more than ever, whenever she feels stressed or upset, she has urges to *act out* violently toward others. A minor argument with Scott, her mother, or an authority figure can trigger urges to violate others or their property. In short, she is using criminal activity and violence to cope with her own turmoil. Her actions bear little relation to the values she held and espoused before choosing Scott as her personal liberator. At this point, Jennifer has virtually no awareness that she has replaced one emotional trap with another.

DEFENSIVE TRAPS

Here's a brief summary of the more common defense mechanisms that can cloud judgment and undermine efforts to treat ourselves and others fairly. They overlap a great deal. To understand how each defense works, imagine that you were raised by a very domineering mother, who, in a well-meaning but suffocating fashion, attempted to control every nuance of your life. In fact, she still does. Nothing you do is good enough or quite right. The last time you tried to set a limit on her encroachments, she became profoundly depressed and wouldn't speak to you for a month. You need her, perhaps too much, and you love her a great deal. But you also can't stand her most of the time and have had dreams of shipping her off to Madagascar. If you can't accept the conflicting thoughts and feelings, you might try to protect yourself from conscious stress by unconsciously altering reality a bit.

The center column in the following Benchmark represents what you might say to yourself to fend off the anxiety and depression that could result if you fully acknowledged the depth of your feelings. If no defenses were operating, you would experience the feeling and accept the truth behind the statement, "Most of the time, I can't stand my mother!"

Some of the defense mechanisms, such as repression, isolation, displacement, rationalization, and reaction formation, can be helpful mediators when used sparingly. They help us cope with personal loss, trauma, humiliations, and difficult situations. My friend's repression of a humiliating incident, wetting his pants, allowed him to return to school and get on with things. He essentially "delayed" the information for later processing as an adult. Because these defenses help us cope, it's often difficult to know when they've ballooned into habitual, distorted ways of relating to ourselves and others.

Unconscious Traps: Defending Yourself

DEFENSE

WHAT I MAY TELL MYSELF	WHAT IT MEANS
1. Repression "I don't know why I'm so upset around her.	Thoughts and feelings are held in memory, beyond awareness.
2. Splitting "I'm so weak and worthless, she's so strong and good."	Polarizing people, feelings, experiences into good and bad.
3. Denial "She's always been a wonderful, self-sacrificing mother."	Refusing to accept things as they are.
4. Projection "I know she secretly hates me. She probably wishes I were dead."	Attributing your own unacknowledged feelings to others.
5. Isolation "She's always been cloying but I don't remember ever being upset about it."	Feelings are repressed in memory while the events remains conscious.
6. Displacement "I hate my boss, always telling me what to do, like I'm a helpless child!"	Redirecting unconscious feelings and thoughts to a safer outlet.
7. Dissociation "I don't feel anything about her blather after awhile. I shut it out."	Emotions are separated and detached from a situation.
8. Acting Out "Every time I see her I feel like getting loaded, doing something outrageous."	Expressing unconscious conflicts in actions rather than words.
9. Rationalization "She's doing the best she can and so am I. What more can be expected?"	Creating a cover story to excuse or water down true motives.
10. Reaction Formation "Mom, come move in with us."	An impulse or feeling is denied and turned into its opposite.

Other defenses, such as splitting, denial, projection, dissociation, and acting out are almost always bad news for adults. All diminish our sense of personal responsibility. When we fall into these traps, even temporarily, we disown a part of ourselves. Rather than facing personal shortcomings, shame, and guilt, we blot them from existence or attribute them to other people. This happens at great cost. Relationships deteriorate and our sense of wholeness is undermined by feelings of emptiness and a relentless sense of dissatisfaction.

Although the latter group of defenses is more troublesome, all the defenses listed have the potential to interfere with the way we handle our moral lives. When clarity of vision is obscured and self-knowledge is denied or avoided, our ability to size up moral situations, reason through moral choices, and carry out positive actions is seriously compromised. Furthermore, our sense of personal goodness can get lost in the storm.

Larger Forces

Most of what we've been talking about so far has focused on individual psychology, the things that go on inside of each of us that can affect our ability to do the right thing. That's extremely important, but it's not enough. We don't live in a vacuum. We're part of families, businesses, communities, nations, and other groups.

Some of the most intractable problems and atrocities of our time are related to group forces. Think of hate groups, corporate fraud, the Holocaust, the slippery things you may do at work. What happens to our judgment, values, and personal responsibility when we join groups? How do we end up doing things we wouldn't ordinarily do? What goes wrong and why? It's time to see.

SEVEN

Powerful Seductions: Losing Yourself at Work and in Groups

It may be outrageous and difficult to understand, but you've seen it all before: The incest continues for years as family members look the other way, a reasonable man finds "the way" and runs off with a destructive cult; an intelligent woman is suckered by a "motivational seminar" claiming she'll make a fortune selling overpriced beauty products; a well-respected corporation suppresses its research findings and continues selling a questionable medication; a government agency violates basic human rights; one country, fueled by religious beliefs, attempts to destroy another.

Standing on the outside, it's fairly easy to see the folly, the misguided assumptions, and the wayward paths. But if you and I can see these things, why can't others? Is it possible that they do see but just don't care? Are they simply lacking in values? Are they questionable people to begin with?

You and I, of course, are independent thinkers. We're far too reasonable, critical, and well-balanced to lose ourselves to a group mentality. Any move in the wrong direction and we would speak up or pull out immediately. Besides, any group we would belong to is different. If only it were so simple.

STRANGE THINGS HAPPEN IN GROUPS

Any number of images may come to mind when we think of group mentality: hooded Klansmen circling around a burning cross, cult rituals that abuse children and animals, inner-city gang shootings, skinheads beating immigrants, a mob killing, the Holocaust, a terrorist bombing. It's easy to put our finger on examples such as these because they seem so extreme, so different, so blatantly evil. These group activities are aimed at harming other people and are contrary to the universal moral values that most people espouse.

While it's vitally important that we find out how and why "other" people join extreme group activities like these, it's even more important to see how "we" are all susceptible to the more subtle group forces that pervade our daily lives. Our families, friends, work situations, spiritual groups, community values, legal and political systems, exert immense pressures that influence our moral choices and actions. In many cases, we may not even be aware that our thinking pattern has shifted away from or compromised our personal values. Group values are not always the same as personal values, yet the boundaries are easily blurred.

It goes without saying that the cohesive power of groups is essential for civilization. We need families and other groups to develop and survive. But our concern here is to explore how good people get caught up in group activities that harm others and stray significantly from the universal moral values cited in chapter 2. Ordinary psychological processes combined with special group forces can override or skew our better judgment and lead to progressively larger transgressions. Our character and resolve are put to the ultimate test in groups. As history has shown, groups have an enormous potential for evil, as well as good. How and why do they engender such power?

Feeling Good in Groups

To illustrate how group influence works on a small scale, think of the last time you were scrutinized and "accepted" by a new group. Perhaps you were anxious in a new job, wanting to please your boss, win the approval of your coworkers, and demonstrate your competency. Regardless of your inner strength, it was a highly charged, demanding situation that required the emotional agility to sense and respond to a thousand little social cues. Like your first date in high school, things were coming at you from all directions and threatening to slip out of your control. At least you were wearing the right shoes.

To feel unknown and "out" is a nerve-racking experience for most people. As your coworkers scrutinize every little thing about you—trying to place you in some mental category—you do the same to them. The psychological gatekeepers and other defense mechanisms are geared up for self-protective action, devouring enormous amounts of emotional energy in the process (see chapters 5 and 6). When emotional energy is significantly diminished, something has to give.

If you're like most people, you make concessions, however small, to alleviate the tension and become more like your coworkers. Emotionally, you want "in." It's safer that way, takes less energy, and is much more rewarding. Getting to know your colleagues, you are more apt to stress similarities than differences. If your new boss happens to mention that she can't stand aggressive people who drive Saabs, you might laugh it away, pushing aside images of your docile, Saab-driving cousin. Or, having no real opinion on the matter, you might agree. What does it hurt, anyway? Maybe she's right.

As you become known and generally accepted by your colleagues and vice versa, a new feeling emerges. You are part of something larger than yourself, which to varying degrees adds another kernel of power and significance to your life. Your individual identity remains intact but it has shifted ever so slightly to include your new group (assuming that you like what you've seen). "I" and "them" becomes "we" and "us."

Protecting "Us"

Since it is now *your* job and *your* place of employment, your psychological gatekeepers and defenses are partially extended to cover the group as well. The boundaries of your newly expanded identity depend upon your need to belong and your general satisfaction with your coworkers. Another department or your company as a whole may or may not be included in your emotional territory. Perhaps you feel loyalty to your department since your colleagues are united in their opposition to unfair management practices. Perhaps the folks in finance all drive Saabs.

Once you have felt out the parameters of your group, however large or small, you consciously and unconsciously invest a part of yourself to maintain and protect the group interest as well as your own. Your investment could be based on the need for power, money, career advancement, and other personal factors, as well as the emotional need to belong. Whatever the reason, *your group identity (and the identity of the entire group) is now susceptible to many of the same biases, self-deceptions, distortions, and unconscious traps that we found in individuals.* Your group identity may progressively influence or override personal values. You might even adhere to one set of values at work and another at home. Later, we'll see how people typically handle such a discrepancy.

Escaping a Part of Yourself

Say you're chosen to work on an important project with nine of your respected colleagues from various departments. The group's goal is to redesign an international marketing plan for your product, a special glue used in making shoes. Each of you is promised a significant bonus depending upon the quality of the report and its timely completion.

Over many grueling weeks of working together like a family you develop a special camaraderie and understanding. Chances are, one person naturally falls into the more dominant role as leader, even if ideas and decisions are shared equally. You find your own role or place in the group; perhaps you smooth over disagreements.

Over time, you know what to expect from each other. As

in a family, faults and minor idiosyncrasies are accepted and tolerated to a certain degree. In addition, there may be unwritten rules of behavior in the group that don't necessarily apply outside the group: Keep things positive, don't obstruct progress, enforce confidentiality, no hanky panky with other group members, don't say anything about hanky panky if it occurs, stand behind the final report, and so on. Since time is of the essence, discussions are focused and succinct.

You may have reservations about some of the rules but you want to get the job done and support your colleagues. Essentially, you've developed a sense of loyalty and group identity. As a member of the important group, you are much more powerful than you were as an individual. Your self-esteem is enhanced. It feels good to share a connection and identity with your colleagues.

For purposes of our example, assume that prior to this project, you were feeling quite frustrated and blocked in your career aspirations. Your title was mundane and you blended into the daily humdrum. Your identity as a member of a group was stagnant and indistinct. You were even beginning to feel the same way at home. Your spouse never said it, but you sensed what he or she was thinking.

Little by little, your self-concept was sinking in doubt and unfulfilled goals. Maybe something about you was indeed ineffectual and weak. But the group has given you an escape from that part of yourself, and perhaps some of your inhibitions as well. You're finding that in spite of your basic humility, you like the feeling of power.

Once again, there is hope. The scene is set for your heavy investment in the group. *You need them more than they really need you.* And whether you're aware of it or not, you are entering a situation ripe for the subtle distortions of "groupthink."

Spreading Responsibility Too Thin

Although the work group is demanding, there's a certain exhilaration and freedom about making decisions that will

have major implications for your company. You are responsible for certain segments of the project, but the overall conclusions and recommendations will be shouldered by the entire group. No one in particular is responsible. If something
goes wrong, as in the Watergate and the Iran-Contra scandals,
fingers can be pointed at any number of interconnected
"causes." Like the ten firing squad members given nine bul-
lets and one blank, all subconsciously feel as if they have a
diminished responsibility.

Because responsibility is spread, you may be less likely
to object or press your concerns when the group veers toward an ethically gray area. Suppose that your company's
product, a glue used in shoe manufacturing, is only marginally profitable in North America and Europe because of certain regulations that require an expensive additive. The additive produces nausea that discourages deliberate sniffing of
the glue's addictive fumes.

After digging through reams of international documents,
you discover that there are no such regulations in Brazil and
Argentina. The group is ecstatic and congratulates you on
your diligent search. Without the additive, the profit margins
are nearly doubled. Aside from a small Brazilian firm that
produces an inferior product, the only major competitor is
another U.S. company that uses the additive in all of its ex-
ports. Your unofficial group leader suggests, "Maybe they
don't know any better. Or maybe South America is of little
interest to them since they're heavily invested in Asia. Whatever the reason, we can really undercut them."

Another member adds, "Perhaps they're concerned about
the addictive potential." Eyes roll and someone exclaims,
"Give me a break! We don't want to hurt anyone, but we're
not responsible for idiots who choose to snort the snuff. Do
you hold liquor manufacturers responsible for alcoholism?
We'll cover the labels with warnings. It's the best we can do.
Are you with us here?" Nothing more is said.

At the moment, you're riding your own high but you're
troubled at the same time. You've been to Rio de Janeiro and

seen kids as young as five congregating in groups, sniffing glue from old soda cans. The stuff is readily available for crafts and other leather work. The kids remain inebriated for hours at a time, carrying their cans with them like baby bottles.

You tentatively raise the issue again, without conveying the extent of your concern. Someone states that it's perfectly legal to market the product in this manner. Another insists that Brazil and Argentina are marginally developed countries with many social ills. "Unfortunately, kids will suffer and look for escape, no matter what we do." The group leader adds, "You saw these kids in a group, but that doesn't mean the problem is widespread. It could have been an isolated problem in that particular community. Besides, they'll still get the untreated stuff from the local manufacturer." Another says, "South American kids are used to that lifestyle. We can't impose our standards and values on them." Someone else adds, "Really, it's up to the parents. Why don't we just print up some educational pamphlets?" The response is immediate and affirmative.

Having jumped the moral hurdle, the group members are enmeshed in a powerful feeling: They can accomplish almost anything. Each member is intelligent and resourceful. The group has become a strong meeting of minds, it seems, greater than any individual mind. Your reservations remain, but the rationale and practical solution are enticing. You respect your colleagues' observations and enjoy the feeling of unanimity. You suppress your own doubts.

After it's decided, you have small pangs of guilt because you didn't press the issue further. You were passive partly out of fear that others might see you as naive and namby-pamby in a "dog-eat-dog world" and partly because you questioned your own concerns. Rather than feeling guilty about your passivity, you finally convince yourself that the decision was right. On another, perhaps subconscious level, you write it off as "their" decision, even though you passively accepted it and gave it little challenge. Your responsibility is diminished, particularly if you should travel to Rio and see another kid with glazed eyes.

Although you may have had doubts, you're now actively defending yourself and the group. You are invested in a course of action that you ordinarily wouldn't have taken. Once started, you'll have to see it through. Your initial re- search—a nearly mindless task of shuffling through pa- pers—has taken on a life of its own. There are moral con- sequences.

GROUPTHINK

Perhaps, in reality, *you* would have been much more vocal in the above situation. Perhaps you would have suggested the search for or development of a different, less costly ad- ditive. The group didn't even consider that possibility. Or perhaps you would have tenaciously argued that the com- pany's reputation was worth more than the immediate bot- tom line. Fairness and ethical responsibility can lead to un- foreseen rewards, even in business.

While most of us assume that we would be stronger in group situations like this, often we aren't. That's because many of the forces operating do so on a very subtle level that's usually beyond our immediate awareness. And this ap- plies to any group that holds part of your emotional invest- ment—family, church, political group, therapy group, profes- sional guild, whatever. *The greater the degree of esprit de corps, the greater the danger that we'll at least partially sus- pend our facilities for critical thinking.*

It happens all the time, even in relatively anonymous groups where the ties are more impersonal or vague. Just think about how alive you may have felt at a rock concert, a political rally, a soccer match, or a critical union meeting. The sense of unified purpose, however brief, is uplifting and contagious. And the anonymity may release all sorts of inhi- bitions, allowing you to do things you ordinarily hold in check. Hoods, such as those worn by the Ku Klux Klan and many inner-city gangs, have the same disinhibiting effect. A blank face bears little responsibility.

Sometimes it feels too good to be critical, guarded, and reasonable. Riding with the wave of power is much more thrilling and dangerous. Sometimes the rock concert deteriorates into rock throwing, the political rally plays on images of scapegoats, the soccer match ends in a bloody brawl, and the union meeting dissolves in selfish demands. The danger is compounded if the group was joined out of frustration, fear, self-protection, or a search for power. In those circumstances, some particularly destructive group defenses kick in. We'll examine them shortly.

Before looking a bit deeper, here are some warning signs of groupthink adapted from the work of psychologist Irving Janis. His research centered on groups that make policy decisions, but the principles apply to any group that makes decisions. Our hypothetical example is loaded with symptoms of groupthink. If you look closely, you'll find them all.

 BENCHMARK NO. 6

Eight Warning Signs of Groupthink

Warning Sign	Subconscious Notion
1. An illusion of invulnerability, leading to excessive optimism.	*If all these bright people agree on this decision, we're bound to succeed.*
2. A belief that the group is inherently moral.	*We're all good people, so whatever we do will be good.*
3. Rationalizing and discounting informations that might lead members to reconsider their decision.	*We're all well-informed people, so our information is better and more extensive than most.*

4. Viewing other groups as stereotypes—they're evil, weak, stupid, etc.

   They're very different from us. They don't think and feel as we do.

5. Self-censorship. Members with doubts don't speak out or press their concerns.

   Everyone else seems to agree, so I'm probably just being too cautious.

6. An illusion that everyone in the group agrees, so the decision must be right.

   It's gone this far and no one is disagreeing, so our thinking is unanimous.

7. Pressuring or questioning the loyalty of anyone who raises too many doubts.

   He doesn't seem committed to our goals and purpose.

8. A self-appointed "mindguard" who protects group illusions and presses for agreement.

   We've been over that before. Everyone else agrees that we're doing the right thing, so let's get on with it.

EVEN GREATER DANGERS

Not all group actions are as structured and contained as a business project. When times are tough and people feel frustrated, threatened, uncertain, and anxious, they join groups or go along with certain social movements to meet more personal needs. If they feel alienated, angry, or powerless, they'll find immense emotional support, an enhanced social identity, and a renewed sense of purpose in groups that seem to reflect their feelings and beliefs. You saw this happening with Jennifer, the fifteen-year-old who used group criminal activity to fill the emptiness she experienced at home.

Sometimes the group activity is very positive and constructive. Other times, since the group may have been born of frustration, anger, and the need for power, the activity is skewed by several dangerous traps. While working for their vision of a better world—the higher ideal—the group members may overlook the welfare of other people or exclude them from their standards of moral treatment. You've seen it in terrorists who treat each other with respect and compassion but blow innocent "others" to bits. That kind of thinking is a hallmark of evil.

Since World War II and the mind-boggling extermination of six million Jews, psychologists such as Ervin Staub at the University of Massachusetts, Herbert Kelman at Harvard University, and many more have searched to make sense of this and other dark mysteries of human destruction. While the reasons may never be fully understood, several important psychological traps have been identified.

These traps, or distortions in thinking, can occur to varying degrees in *any* group. Whether they explode into unbridled destruction depends upon numerous complex factors. But we can learn to spot the traps before they ever reach that stage.

BENCHMARK NO. 7

DANGEROUS TRAPS FOR GROUPS

1. **Us and Them:** We organize reality with categories. Trivial differences—looks, clothing, speech, preferences, etc.—are often used to place people into groups. It's easy to assume subconsciously that people in such a group are all of one mind. They may be categorized as an outgroup or, in the extreme, as the enemy.

2. **They're Inferior:** Once placed in an outgroup, people are seen as undesirable and inferior in certain aspects. This raises our self-esteem and sense of superiority. People in the outgroup are more likely

to be treated as objects who don't feel as we do. They risk being excluded from our values of humane treatment.

3. **Blaming Others:** The causes behind our problems are seldom clear-cut. In our frustration, it's easy to oversimplify and blame others. Getting rid of or changing others provides a tangible but illusory solution. It makes us feel as if our problems can be controlled. Our own responsibility is diminished.

4. **They Must Deserve Their Plight:** Once we devalue and blame others, we're more likely to assume that some weakness in their character, intelligence, or morals has led to their plight. They've brought it on themselves. We may erroneously believe that the world is just—people get what they deserve. This makes it easier for us to accept their suffering.

5. **Anything for the Cause:** Causes are often based upon a certain set of ideals. Sometimes the ideals take the form of intellectual dogma and rhetoric. The ideals promise a better world. Immersed in rhetoric, we're more apt to scapegoat other people for getting in the way of our cause. Hurting others feels justified.

6. **"I Was Just Following Orders":** As part of a mission or job, we assume that the authorities who give us the orders are operating with a larger sense of purpose. The mission is so important that everyday morality and law don't apply. It can make us feel justified and important. A new morality, based on obligation, overrides our values.

7. **A Routine Process:** Once involved in a job or mission, there is pressure to continue. As we're immersed in the small daily tasks involved, we're apt

to focus on their completion rather than on their larger meaning. We stop asking questions, fill out forms, and go about our business. The little steps become normal and routine.

8. **Mental Compartments:** Remember how people, to varying degrees, can "split off" a part of themselves? The same process can occur when we are engaged in group activities that initially conflict with our values. We push the conflict aside, focus on tasks, or make excuses. If this goes on long enough, we may come to accept the behavior or convince ourselves that they have a larger, moral purpose.

Who's at Risk?

We're all at risk of falling into these traps, but some of us are more susceptible than others. Some people are highly committed to group activities that support their particular values, but at the same time they are able to maintain an objective, independent view of the group's conduct. Others, regardless of their intelligence, tend to lose themselves in the group.

For the latter, the emotional or practical need for identifying with the group obscures the boundary between personal and group identity. Slowly but surely, one small step leads to another as personal values are submerged in group morality. Something insignificant, such as wearing a certain article of clothing, accepting a favor, or helping another member, can be a small catalyst for further involvement and commitment. Unfortunately, even if the group activity is initially positive, the susceptible person's vision is compromised. He or she may not be able to detect a subtle shift toward the traps cited above.

Some people such as Eric, the assistant manager who physically abuses his wife, are raised in authoritarian families that stress obedience and give little attention to the development of empathy. In Eric's case, although he is often rebellious around authority, he's a prime candidate for group activities that play on frustration and promise personal power. Since he has a diminished sense of personal responsibility and empathy, he's likely to ferret out scapegoats and treat them with great contempt. And since his family condoned violence as a way of resolving conflicts (his father, you may remember, was also physically abusive), it's highly probable, given his controlling, rigid personality, that he would support group activities that devalue and mistreat others. The morality of humane treatment would not apply to those whom he sees as inferior.

In a similar manner, Jennifer, the pregnant fifteen-year-old, is a perfect candidate for destructive groupthink. Although she has a good capacity for empathy, her ability to turn off or push her feelings and conflicting values into mental compartments sets the scene for uninhibited, hurtful behavior. As you have seen, she learned to dissociate or withdraw from her feelings as a way of dealing with the erratic behavior of her alcoholic mother. Jennifer's troubled home situation left her with deep-seated, unmet needs for acceptance, approval, and release of frustration, needs that now fuel her commitment to Scott and his group. Once involved, it's extremely difficult for her to challenge or break with the group values. To do so would be quite painful and possibly dangerous.

But not everyone who falls prey to group mentality has deep-seated psychological conflicts. Richard, you may remember, is the nineteen-year-old son of David, the attorney having the extramarital affair. Richard is attending a prestigious technical institute and is barely passing his courses, (see page 16 for his version of the story). Except for his academic problems at school and his concern about his preoccupied father, he is relatively happy and well adjusted. But he is on the verge of failing an electrical engineering course. Spurred on by students who have obtained a copy of a major exam in the course, Richard is considering cheating. "So many people are doing it, it's like, if I don't, I'll be screwed, at the bottom of the heap. My future is at stake here." Given his father's tendency to instill a "winners and losers" world-view and his family's great investment in his education, Richard is under enormous pressure. He knows better than to cheat, but the group may provide the impetus and ratio-nale to compromise his values. (You'll see what he actually chooses to do in chapter 9.)

In short, individual circumstances, stressful situations, cultural or family norms, and the way we view the world can all raise our susceptibility to groupthink. What we choose to do and how far we go with it depends upon our personality, our character, and the strength of our values.

PART II

FINDING YOUR WAY: PATHS AND PITFALLS

EIGHT

Overcoming Moral Blindness: Lighting the Shadows

As you have seen in Part I of this book, the path we forge through the moral maze is ultimately quite personal and unique. Whether we get through the maze depends upon many factors, including our character and personality, our understanding of moral values, and our ability to reason through moral choices. In this and the next several chapters, you'll discover some important tools for navigating the moral maze and enriching your life—without becoming a "moralizing" bore.

First things first. Long before any moral decisions are made, we must be able to recognize when our psychological conflicts are embedded in moral issues and when our everyday actions are likely to influence, hurt, or help other people. Without truly seeing and feeling, without a sharply honed sensitivity to moral issues, it is impossible to effectively resolve our personal conflicts or plan constructive actions.

THE IMPORTANCE OF MORAL SENSITIVITY

Whenever you sort through a complex issue from your past or wrangle with a dilemma in a present relationship, it's likely that you're juggling all sorts of moral questions. Whether you see the moral dimensions of your problem depends upon your level of moral awareness, your *moral sensitivity.*

Perhaps you still feel depressed about something that

happened in the past. You've been over it a thousand times in your head, using your best psychological understanding and insight, but you still have a nagging sense that something is missing from the equation. If your dilemma involves other people, there's a good possibility that you have avoided or not carefully considered the moral issues involved. *Did I do what was right? Who was to blame? How much was my fault? Should I forgive? Is he or she a good person? Am I a good person? Should I do something to make up for this?*

Questions of morality must always come into play in order to justly hold other people accountable, determine your own level of responsibility, forgive yourself or others, or change your harmful ways. And if you're making a difficult decision in your life at present, you must be able to determine and even predict, to the best of your ability, how your actions might affect other people. This skill lies at the heart of moral sensitivity

Moral sensitivity tells you when your actions or those of others have moral implications. In all aspects of human relationships, your moral sensitivity should be as sharp and clear as possible. To keep it finely honed, *you must be able to feel the pain of other people, place yourself in their shoes, and be aware of larger values that may go beyond your immediate needs and desires.* Moral sensitivity alone can't tell you the right thing to do. But your sensitivity will help illuminate past and present shadows and clarify what the stakes are for all involved.

Wayward Paths: Diversions and Distractions

As you surely know all too well, people differ greatly in their ability to understand themselves, size up complex situations, and predict the effects of their actions. Some are quite sensitive and very astute in understanding the feelings, motives, and needs of other people. Their moral sensitivity is finely tuned. Others, in spite of obvious intelligence, need to be hit over the head with obvious signs of suffering before

they get the picture. But we all experience varying degrees
of insensitivity and moral blindness from time to time. As
you saw in chapter 4, we may be very astute in one situation
and oblivious or selectively blind in another. A host of psychological and perceptual factors may lead us astray.

Strong Emotions, Lack of Self-Knowledge, Skewed Perceptions

Emotions lie at the core of our moral sensitivity, but they
can also dull the edge. Loaded situations trigger strong emotional reactions that can color perceptions, overwhelm reason, and lead to self-deception and poor judgment. *It's easy
to misinterpret or selectively ignore moral implications when
we're immersed in anxiety, anger, fear, hate, or even love.*
The same holds true when we are self-absorbed or indiffer-
ent. We are not as likely to see what we don't want to see.
But whether we are apathetic or thrown off course by strong
emotion, the result can be the same. We divert, block, or turn
off our capacity to feel or to anticipate the pain of others.
Moral sensitivity, then, is greatly enhanced with a heavy
dose of self-awareness—knowledge of emotional vulnerabilities, biases, and strengths.

The chain linking our emotions and perceptions to our
moral sensitivity is quite complex. It is often difficult to pin-
point what has gone wrong when we fail to act or react with
caring and empathy. Sometimes our moral sensitivity appears to be blunted when, in fact, we're having problems *interpreting an ambiguous situation.* Last summer, my wife
and I were lying on the grassy banks of the Charles River in
Boston when we saw two young men off in the distance tus-
sling on the grass. They jumped to their feet, yelled at each
other, and scuffled again. Now, this sort of thing happens all
the time in a university town like Boston—young people
yelling, screaming bloody murder, wrestling in mock anger,
dissolving in laughter. In time, most of us pay little attention
to it. On that particular day, after a brief moment of concern,

this is what we did—along with at least fifty other people trying to ignore the scene.

It turned out that one young man was brutally bashing the other on the chest with a hammer. And we had done nothing. The reality of the situation escaped us because it was totally unexpected and alien. Had one person in the crowd interpreted it differently, perhaps all of us might have been moved to action. On the other hand, the not-so-subtle pangs of guilt I'm experiencing while writing this raise the ugly possibility that I didn't "see" the attack because to do so would have put me at risk and disrupted a nice day. Perish the thought.

In situations like these, where we fail to see or respond to the misfortune of others, our moral sensitivity, or lack of it, will be influenced by our perceptions, the social context in which the events occur, and even our past experiences. Ellen and Martin Greenberg, two dear friends of mine, heard the now-infamous cries of Kitty Genovese as she was brutally murdered in 1964 in Kew Gardens, a neighborhood in Queens, New York City. The case was highly publicized because thirty-eight neighbors apparently did not intervene or call the police when Ms. Genovese repeatedly cried out, over a long time, as she was being stabbed. The incident came to symbolize an unconscionable moral apathy, self-absorption, and unwillingness to become involved. Ellen Greenberg, who is still haunted by the victim's wail and the media's condemnation, provides her perspective of what happened:

It is very hard to refute the newspaper accounts of our indifference without it sounding like a litany of excuses. That people did not answer her cry for help is unconscionable, but the media's vilification of those of us who lived there wasn't good, either. The reporters made no attempt to understand the neighborhood.

Like our neighbors in Kew Gardens, we lived on

a canyon street of four-story apartment buildings. Each apartment had a screened-in terrace overlooking the street. We could sit out and look across at people looking across at us. We always felt like it was a safe place. On the night of the murder, I was lifted out of sleep. The room was dark; it took a few seconds to determine why I'd wakened. There was an eerie wailing sound that seemed to be floating up from the street. It sounded like Irish keening, a long wailing lament for the dead. Martin awoke and asked what it was. "It sounds like keening." The sound faded and in a few minutes we were both back to sleep.

In the morning we learned that we'd been listening to Kitty Genovese dying. I called our friends in the building opposite the parking lot and now of small shops where she had been attacked. They too had heard the wail, checked their infant son, found him asleep, and gone back to bed.

The next day, the street was full of people and cars, coming to look at the bloodstains on the sidewalk; and coming to look at us, the people the newspapers said had not gone to Kitty's aid. But things were not so simple or clear.

In the first place, on weekends it was not unusual to hear fights outside the local bar, which was near the murder scene. Yells, breaking of glass, were part of the sounds to that we were inured. Like us, most people were probably awakened to the last of Kitty's cries. No actual words were audible; just that awful moan that had no context. Very few who heard it had windows overlooking the scene. Even had we gotten out of bed and looked, we'd have seen nothing.

In the second place, a large refugee population lived in the area, most especially in the building opposite the bar. It was not unusual to hear people conversing in a foreign language, often German. Some had numbers tattooed on their arms. Some were afraid of the police. Some probably had had their own cries for help ignored. Some lived by the credo "Don't get involved." How seeing what was happening did not lead them to forget their fears and call the police is a mystery or perhaps a true measure of their past experience. Contrary to the media reports, all who lived there were not "bad" people.

Lack of Knowledge, Consequences Far Removed

Sometimes our moral sensitivity is blunted because we may not be very sophisticated about politics, interpersonal psychology, or the ways of the world in general. We may *lack crucial information* and fail to see the complex chain of events that could be triggered by our actions. At other times the *consequences of our actions may seem too far removed to consider*—buying that exotic fur, dumping engine oil in the river, or selling inferior products. Momentary gratification blinds us to the long-term consequences. Or we may not realize that we are hurting others, for example, by voting for a new highway that will bypass and devastate a small town. And sometimes we simply can't predict what all the effects of our actions might be.

Regardless of all the factors that can confuse and obscure our moral sensitivity, we have a responsibility to learn as much as we can about ourselves, the needs and feelings of other people, the pressing moral issues of our time, and the practical realities of functioning in a political world. We can't know and predict everything, but our ignorance does not diminish the consequences of our actions.

CLOSER TO HOME: FEAR OF "JUDGING"

Fear of judging can also blunt our moral sensitivity, particularly in close relationships. Throughout Part I of this book, we examined the psychological and moral elements in the lives of Eric and Vanessa. As you remember, Eric emotionally browbeats and physically abuses Vanessa, his wife. He blames Vanessa for his failures and hides inadequacy under a cloak of bravado and control, something he learned from his own abusive father. Vanessa is steeped in denial of Eric's behavior and her own role in perpetuating a bad situation. Part of Vanessa's difficulty is related to her reluctance to cast "judgments," as we will see in the following incident.

After Vanessa reluctantly canceled an important evening out with a close friend, the friend asked her if she thought Eric's controlling behavior was wrong. Vanessa took a quick, well-practiced sidestep: "He had a lousy day at work and wanted me to be there for him. That's Eric. He's a royal pain, but he needs me. How can I say that it's wrong? I'm certainly not perfect, so it's not for me to judge."

The fact is that Vanessa had been in tears over the canceled plans. She had looked forward to getting out of the house, sharing warm feelings with her friend, filling the emotional void she experiences with Eric. The saddest part is that she believed every word of the excuse she had tailored for her friend. Vanessa could not allow herself to be judgmental. And in the process, she once again stifled her feelings and her moral sensitivity.

Judgmental. It sounds like a nasty word. Isn't it reserved for moralistic cranks who bolster their egos by playing God? How can a person be judgmental and retain humility? But a better question might be, How can a person live in the world and make choices without making moral judgments about human *behavior?*

Let's be honest about this: Although we may couch our observations in other terms, we make judgments about people and their activities all the time. *If we jump to conclusions based on prejudice, bias, and lack of information, we are in fact being judgmental in the worst sense of the word.* Nevertheless, we are living in a world that requires us to make judgments about our own and other people's *deeds.* To do so is quite dangerous, yet the alternatives may be far worse. Lines must be drawn, judgments must be reached.

Vanessa's friend asked her if she thought Eric's controlling behavior was wrong. She wasn't asking for an assessment of his soul. Yet Vanessa, in her humility, thought she
was being virtuous by avoiding a moral judgment. Like
Vanessa, many of us are very hesitant to judge the behavior
of those we're closest to or depend upon. Instead, we make
excuses: "He's mean because he's overworked; she lies to
keep the peace; he manipulates everyone to get his way but
that's just how he is; she's a bitch because she was abused
by her father; he's involved with a gang and hurts others because he's afraid." In our avoidance, we may be creating
emotional straitjackets and perpetuating negative cycles.

Rekindling Moral Sensitivity in Relationships

While being cautious and objective is certainly the wisest
path to take in "judging" others, there may be huge practical
and psychological consequences if we continually dance
around ethical issues in relationships. Vanessa learned the
dance many years ago with her own domineering father and
passive mother, and now she's carrying on the tradition with
her husband, Eric. Because of this, she is depriving herself of
the ability to size up the limits of her own responsibility,
make positive choices, and grow beyond her present conflicts. She's also setting a bad example for their two-year-old
son. Furthermore, how can she hold Eric accountable and in-
sist on change if she makes no judgments about his behavior?

Vanessa is sitting on years and years of unexpressed
anger, frustration, and disappointment. Her self-esteem is
abysmal, and she habitually assumes the blame when things
go wrong. Her judgments are always directed toward herself.
She's harboring shame and guilt for the bad deeds of other
people. Unfortunately, these feelings will continue to accu-
mulate until she allows herself to see the moral picture and
re-experience the outrage that she blunted years ago. Forgiveness, if due, can come later.

Two Important Questions

A very simple question might cut through Vanessa's moral insensitivity about Eric's behavior, her father's manipulations, and her mother's passivity: *Would you treat other people the way these people have treated you?* Most likely she would respond, "I could never hurt anyone like that. It would be *wrong* if I did." The doors would open to the past and allow her to confront some family illusions.

Perhaps she would feel what she has been holding at bay for years. Perhaps she would see her own passivity and how it's affecting her son. By evaluating and judging according to universal values such as the Incredible Seven (fairness, caring, responsibility, respect, honesty, loyalty, and liberty), Vanessa could begin to free herself emotionally and develop realistic plans for her life. As you saw in chapter 4, she could compile a Values Profile to see where her life is out of balance. A Values Profile is an informal snapshot of how a person relates to the world in a moral sense. It covers each of the levels of interaction described above (self, intimate relationships, family, friends, job, community, country, and society in general) and examines the values followed or aspired to on each level. (See Eric's profile beginning on page 73 and Vanessa's on page 76).

In a similar manner, Eric needs to address the right and wrong of his father's physically abusive behavior, as well as his own. He must deal with the past, or it will distort the future. His anger and outrage will continue to be directed toward innocent people rather than at the source of his turmoil.

If he can't respond to the central question asked of Vanessa, perhaps another simple question might open the doors and stimulate moral sensitivity: *Would you like to be treated the way you treat Vanessa?* This question, like Vanessa's, may seem simplistic and obvious. But people lose sight of both questions all the time.

I'M RIGHT, YOU'RE WRONG

Vanessa's situation is easier to size up than many since it involves physical abuse and other blatantly harmful behavior. Our moral sensitivity is readily sparked because there are few gray areas to confuse thinking and dampen our feelings. But most of our dilemmas and conflicts are more subtle. The ethical elements are harder to define and tease out as we become entangled in who's right and who's wrong.

When we've been hurt or feel that we've been treated unfairly, it's very easy to fall into a petty game of blaming and defensiveness. *Rather than looking at larger principles and values, we may mistakenly see something as wrong simply because it makes us feel bad or impedes our personal desires.*

The larger question—whether an actual injustice has been committed—often gets lost in the heat of the moment. We're apt to feel angry, hurt, and possibly betrayed long before our moral sense of right and wrong has a chance to kick in. This makes it even more difficult to resolve the conflict. Since each party feels aggrieved and argues solely from self-interest, the risk of missing the forest for the trees is enormous. Inevitably, there will be a million little reasons why the other party is wrong.

Larger Values and the Observing Judge

To cut through the morass of self-interest, hurt feelings, and power struggles, it is often helpful to pull back a bit and assume the role of the Observing Judge. This is easier said than done, but it's a step in the right direction. *The Observing Judge looks at the situation according to what is right rather than who is right.* From this broader perspective, relevant values from the Incredible Seven can be used as general guidelines.

Without a doubt, even if you and another party try to be objective, there will be disagreements concerning whether a particular value or personal right has been violated. But, at a minimum, this approach has the potential to move the focus from emotional claims to a more reasoned discussion. Since the discussion focuses on universal guidelines outside the person, defenses and excuses may not interfere as much.

For example, much of Eric's behavior is based on the assumption that he has a right to impose his needs and wishes on Vanessa. He may not even be aware that he's operating from this belief. If anything, he might claim that it is wrong for Vanessa to visit her friends without him. Given Vanessa's background, she might be condoning this belief on some level, even though it leads to her unhappiness.

Without necessarily being critical or blaming, the Observing Judge position opens the door for a discussion about the meaning of liberty, equality, respect, fairness, and other values. In spite of Eric's psychological problems, perhaps he can learn that adults in relationships aren't normally entitled to control each other. Perhaps Vanessa can learn that she must take responsibility for changing her situation, however difficult change may be.

Many of our daily squabbles and major conflicts center on basic assumptions concerning what is right. The problem is, we're often too close and involved to see them. And even if we do recognize that a larger question is at stake, we may not have any guidelines for comparison. That's why the values found in the Incredible Seven (justice or fairness, caring, respect, responsibility, honesty, loyalty, and liberty) are so important. Knowing and understanding them is an essential part of moral sensitivity.

BLAMING AND FORGIVING

What happens when our moral sensitivity sharpens and we uncover moral transgressions from the past, either in ourselves or others? Do we live our lives blaming others for our difficulties? Or do we simply forgive and be done with it? How do we know when it's time to forgive? If we're the perpetrator, do we simply try to live with our guilt? Do we make apologies for our bad deeds and leave it at that? What difference does all this make anyhow?

As our moral sensitivity increases, we're often able to see things in a different light. While the light illuminates the moral elements of our conflicts, it also forces us to deal with the questions raised above. Handling issues of blame and forgiveness requires an ability to sort through the various levels of responsibility and decide whether to hold ourselves or others accountable.

If we have unjustly hurt others, we must decide to live with the guilt, if any, or make apologies and amends in some way. If we feel we've been unjustly hurt, we must determine whether we want to forgive others. Forgiveness is a very special act that essentially says, *"You are truly sorry for what you've done. We both know it was wrong. While it was hurtful, I will no longer hold it against you. We're all fallible at times."*

Obstacles to Effective Forgiveness

Forgiveness is a powerful equalizer: It helps free the victim of the bitterness and anger that eats away at the spirit while at the same time liberating the perpetrator from much of his or her guilt. It allows all involved a better chance to get on with their lives. But because it is so powerful, it cannot be dispensed lightly. Some people are far too free with their forgiveness, seeing it as a magical curative that will take bad feelings away.

Eric apologizes and begs for Vanessa's forgiveness every time he physically abuses her. Vanessa, the eternally "good" person, feels virtuous and nurturing every time she forgives him. But the situation is getting worse rather than better. Eric's remorse is fleeting and stems from a fear of losing his partner rather than any moral sense. Vanessa's forgiveness is superficial and allows her to avoid the real issues. There is nothing virtuous about this kind of forgiveness.

For forgiveness to have any impact, it must be given freely after a careful and compassionate assessment of responsibility. It cannot be coerced or used to avoid deeper concerns. Furthermore, it is most effective when given in response to sincere, heartfelt remorse. And sometimes it cannot be given at all. *Sometimes a person is hurt too much to allow the sense of equality and shared vulnerability that is inherent in forgiveness.* Only he or she can make that difficult decision.

Some people like Jennifer, the fifteen-year-old girl involved in housebreaks and other criminal activities, have never learned what apology and forgiveness are all about. Jennifer's mother, the successful real estate agent and closet alcoholic, was so immersed in shame and secret guilt about her dependency that her daily indiscretions toward her daughter seemed insignificant. She projected her own difficulties on Jennifer and punished her with little or no justification.

Steeped in false pride, she seldom offered a sincere apology for her own mistakes and certainly would not accept Jennifer's timid apologies. Other times, she would force Jennifer to apologize for things that weren't her fault. Jennifer learned to see the world as a place where people aren't truly held accountable for their actions, where apologies are so many words, and forgiveness is empty.

For Jennifer, existence feels like a no-win situation. When mistakes are made, she sees no way to deal with her remorse, make amends, and move on with her life. Instead, she turns her feelings off and rationalizes her behavior. The negative part of her self snowballs, while the good part seems irrelevant.

Remember Shana? Shana is the twenty-seven-year-old legal assistant having an affair with David, her married boss. She has some serious personality problems that undermine her moral vision and lead to pervasive feelings of emptiness. (See page 105 for an exploration of her psychological difficulties.) Shana's sense of right and wrong is based on whatever relieves her pain and fills the emptiness for the moment.

Shana also has great difficulty with apology and forgiveness because her sense of personal responsibility lacks a firm core. Whenever she is hurting or something thwarts her desires, she immediately looks outward rather than inward. "If I feel bad, it's because someone is doing something bad to me." Left to her own devices, she is largely incapable of evaluating the spectrum of responsibility—a necessary step in forgiveness.

For Shana, apology and forgiveness are little more than practical manipulations to meet her own needs. Perhaps with therapy she would be able to sort through the convoluted tangle of responsibility and unacknowledged guilt that stems from her incestuous family situation. In a way, her sense of moral responsibility would have to be rediscovered and rebuilt, step by step.

At some point in the process, Shana would need to decide whether to confront those who hurt her. As these things often go, her stepfather left the scene long ago and is not available to face his victim. Shana is left holding the bag. Since an apology from him is not forthcoming, an important step for Shana would be to look at her hidden guilt, determine how much of it, if any, is justified, and forgive the acts of a desperate child. Such honesty plays an essential role in recovering the good person within.

Shana might also choose to forgive her stepfather, but in a more limited way. She can never experience the liberation of receiving his heartfelt apology, seeing his remorse, and deciding whether it warrants forgiveness. But she can try to *understand* why he did what he did without necessarily *excusing* him. Psychological explanations and explorations of family dynamics should never serve as easy excuses, but they can help make sense of our fallibility. With understanding, Shana can decide whether she wants to let go of her unhealthy hatred and anger toward this fallible human being.

Confronting her mother might also prove to be difficult. Chronically depressed and suffering from a variety of physical problems, Shana's mother might appear to be too vulnerable to handle the truth. Shana may be afraid to open old wounds. But by protecting her mother, Shana could miss an important healing process that both desperately need. Subconscious guilt is a key ingredient in certain types of depression. Perhaps her mother knows far more than Shana suspects.

Is Sorry Enough?

Prisons are full of people who may be truly sorry, and courts are jammed with lawsuits even though sincere apologies have been offered. When laws are broken or rights have been legally violated, society identifies the perpetrators and determines the nature and length of the punishment. When people step over the line, punishment is a part of justice. Simply being sorry doesn't cut it.

When laws are not involved, we're left to our own devices to determine when an apology is sufficient. With few guidelines, that can be very difficult. Without a jury to help decide, we may not even agree on who is responsible for what. Forgiveness, in those instances, may amount to a shared truce in which mutual apologies are offered and accepted. We agree to stop punishing each other.

When No One Listens or Forgives

What does a person—a perpetrator—do when his or her sincere apology falls on deaf ears? Sometimes, hearing "I'm deeply sorry" doesn't have much effect on a victim, even if some other form of punishment has been invoked. The hurt has been too great. In those cases, or cases where the victims are many or faceless, the perpetrator may be left with the hopeless feeling that nothing can ever be done to make up for bad or questionable deeds. If he or she has moral under-pinnings, the guilt may be paralyzing.

In those instances, apologizing repeatedly does little more than intensify feelings of shame and humiliation. As anyone who has ever attended a Twelve-Step program such as Alcoholics Anonymous knows, apology alone is not suffi-cient. To recover the good person within, amends must be made, if not directly to those who have been hurt, then to the community at large. This can take the form of helping others, contributing services, working for worthy causes, im-proving relationships, becoming a better person, and so forth.

A Values Profile, as shown in chapter 4, can be particu-larly helpful in determining where amends should be made. The Values Profile shows how the Incredible Seven have been applied, neglected, or overlooked in each level of a per-son's life—self, intimate relationships, friends, job, commu-nity, and so forth. When values are grossly out of balance or greatly contradict each other from level to level, problems such as anxiety, depression, guilt, and moral confusion can result.

THE PRICE

As you have seen, honing your moral sensitivity does not come without a price. When you become aware, you can no longer cater to your impulses, cast responsibility to the wind, or behave as if your actions have no consequences. (Except on vacation . . . within reason, of course.) You must also wade through the murky realms of responsibility and decide when apologies and forgiveness are in order. Even worse, now that you sense that certain actions may have moral consequences, you have to determine which actions are better than others and decide what you're going to do, the subject of the next chapter. Life used to be so easy.

Before going on, here's a summary of tips discussed in this chapter.

BENCHMARK NO. 8

TIPS FOR HONING YOUR MORAL SENSITIVITY

1. Before taking a course of action, try to place yourself in the other person's shoes.

2. Pay attention to your emotional responses. Do not numb, ignore, or talk away uncomfortable feelings.

3. Know and understand universal moral values such as the Incredible Seven: justice or fairness, caring, respect, responsibility, honesty, loyalty, and liberty.

4. Look at a course of action or a conflict from as many different angles as you can. Get as much information as possible.

5. Consider, to the best of your ability, the short- and long-term consequences of your actions. Who might be harmed? Try to look beyond the immediate circumstances.

6. Be aware of your own vulnerabilities and biases—qualities that may block feelings of empathy or cloud your judgment. Self-knowledge is crucial for moral sensitivity.

7. Use reason, honesty, and compassion to help determine who is responsible for what. Strong feelings such as anxiety, hate, anger, and fear can distort perceptions.

8. To help determine whether your own behavior may be wrong, ask yourself, "Would I like to be treated the way I'm treating others?" Before making excuses for other people, you might ask, "Would I treat them the way they are treating me?"

9. It helps to look at situations through the broad perspective of the Observing Judge. Step back and use larger values as guidelines. Try to determine *what is right* rather than who is right. Defensive squabbles and blaming might be defused.

10. Apology and forgiveness are powerful liberators that should not be taken lightly. Meaningful forgiveness is most effective when given in response to sincere, heartfelt remorse. It is a freely chosen option for the person who has been harmed.

11. Use a Values Profile (see chapter 4) to help determine how you relate to the world in a moral sense. You may find areas where amends would be liberating.

NINE

Moral Headaches:
What's the Right Thing to Do?

There's no escaping it now. Once you're aware that your actions may significantly affect other people, you have to make
some ethical, moral choices. And you can't always get off the
hook by ignoring the situation. That, too, is an ethical choice
that could have great implications.

Our lives are filled with moral choices and decisions, the
majority of which are so small and automatic that we take
them for granted. Most of us pay the cashier on the way out
of a store, not to avoid punishment, but simply because we
know that stealing is unfair and wrong. But we don't give it
a second thought. *Not stealing* has become a moral habit, a
decision that was made long ago and added to our conscience.

But some of our moral choices are not so simple or clear
cut. Even though we may have great empathy for others and
a healthy conscience, what happens when we're faced with
those disconcerting gray areas? What happens when there
appear to be valid arguments on many sides of an issue?
What if well-meaning, morally sensitive people disagree
about the right thing to do? And what good are values such
as the Incredible Seven if people can't agree on which ones
are the most important in a particular situation?

You're right. We're entering a quagmire here. But that's
the essence of many difficult moral dilemmas: There are no
universally right answers. And in many complex situations,
*if you look for the right thing to do—as if it were a recipe in
a moral cookbook—you'll be sorely disappointed.* Even if

you're of good character and armed with principles and values, *you* must decide which ones you care about most and how they are to be applied. If it's your dilemma, no one can really solve it for you. Others can offer valuable wisdom and guidelines, but the path is ultimately yours to *create.* That seems to be the nature of our existence.

So what do we do? Throw our hands up in resignation? Lie to ourselves that it's all relative and doesn't matter anyway? There is no magic formula for solving complex moral dilemmas—and I won't insult you by promising one here— but there are some important things you should know about our *moral reasoning process* and how it works.

Knowing the basics about moral reasoning can help you understand and sort through difficult dilemmas. It might also help you think about old conflicts in a new light. As a first step, we'll take a look at this information and combine it with a basic framework for making moral decisions. Then we'll wade through some of the dilemmas posed by the players in our moral theater.

HOW WE THINK ABOUT RIGHT
AND WRONG

Back in chapter 3, I briefly touched on moral reasoning, a key ingredient in moral development. Moral reasoning refers to our capacity to understand why some actions may be morally better than others. In conjunction with our feelings, it helps each of us see the rights and needs of others, sort through the values at stake, and determine what we *ought* to do.

Our capacity for moral reasoning develops along a line similar to that of our general reasoning ability. As our general reasoning ability expands during the first two decades of life, we're increasingly able to see more of the factors involved in a complex problem and how they may be related to each other.

An insurmountable problem that you faced at age six may be nothing to you now as an adult. At age six, your perspective was very limited, you generalized (kids with red hair are mean), and you couldn't always tell what was causing what (Daddy is leaving Mommy because I get sick too much). Your experience, your knowledge, and relative mental development limited your problem-solving ability.

The same holds true for our moral reasoning. As it matures, we are able to see and consider larger and larger spheres of influence extending beyond ourselves to family, society, and human rights in general. We learn that right and wrong are not simple matters based on selfish needs. Depending upon the extent of our maturity, we may be able to see and truly *understand* the importance of treating others fairly, why cooperation and just laws are necessary for civilization, and how certain basic human rights override those set by any single society or group.

To cite an example of moral reasoning from chapter 3, if we ask a seven-year-old why it's wrong to steal, he's likely to say, "It's not good to steal because you get in trouble" or "If you steal from someone, they might steal from you." His idea of right and wrong is limited to himself and the immediate consequences. Ask a mature teenager the same question and she might add another dimension—"It's wrong. If everybody went around stealing, society would fall apart."

The seven-year-old reasons correctly, but his answer is more limited. He doesn't get the broader picture. The teenager may agree with his reasoning but she also sees reasons that go beyond punishment or tit-for-tat consequences. She sees the larger implications and understands that certain rules are needed for social cooperation. On the other hand, if she had been raised in an environment where little heed was paid to thinking through moral issues, it's probable that her vision and understanding, like that of the seven-year-old, would be more limited.

It's clear that people differ greatly in their capacity to comprehend, size up, and sort through moral dilemmas. Although age, intelligence, and education are related to the process, we all know overeducated geniuses who are moral idiots. Their vision of the world is limited to their own needs and self-interests. Effective moral thinking, then, requires a combination of ingredients, including:

- a broad perspective that extends beyond our own immediate needs,
- the knowledge and deep understanding of universal values,
- the ability to place ourselves in other people's shoes,
- the give-and-take experience of successful relationships, and
- the well-practiced, lifelong effort to think through moral conflicts.

Some people never really grow beyond the moral reasoning level of the seven-year-old. Others regress to lower levels in stressful situations. Still others spew all sorts of moral rhetoric but choose to behave in a totally self-serving manner. *Our moral reasoning capacity does not in any way guarantee that we will actually behave morally.* But if it's underdeveloped or stuck on a low level, we could be headed for trouble.

What's Your Level of Moral Reasoning?

Although psychologists argue about the existence of separate stages in the development of our moral reasoning, it's helpful to look at the general thinking levels that people tend to fall into when deciding right and wrong. Each level has its own criterion of what is right and why it should be followed. Each is really a way of seeing and thinking about the world. Some people are capable of reasoning on all levels but are inconsistent in everyday application. Others get stuck and can't see or understand the level above.

Before looking at the levels of moral reasoning, it's important to note that people thinking on the same level may arrive at very different conclusions. The levels don't provide cut-and-dried answers, even though the underlying thinking process and perspective may be similar.

Level 1: It's Right If You Don't Get in Trouble

This is the most basic way of thinking. People who operate exclusively in this moral mind-set avoid doing wrong simply to avoid punishment. Consequences alone determine whether an action is right or wrong. If such a person finds a loophole in the law and successfully scams other people, the hurtful acts may be seen as part of a legitimate business. He or she has done nothing wrong. The needs and interests of other people are either ignored or assumed to be the same as those of the perpetrator.

Level 2: Protect Your Own Self-Interest

People immersed in this level of thinking have a better understanding of the give-and-take of relationships and recognize a certain tit-for-tat justice. They realize that cooperation and compromise are necessary to get what they want. But they will follow rules and make agreements only when it's in their best interest. The rules have no moral value. If they're broken, the price is paid, and the game simply continues. Other concerns, such as the community, society, or the environment, are of little interest unless they play a part in their immediate goals. Unfortunately, a very large segment of our population operates primarily from this perspective.

Level 3: Your Personal Relationships Are Everything. Do What Others Expect of You

These individuals decide right and wrong by placing themselves in the other person's shoes. They try to treat others as they themselves wish to be treated and are very concerned about other people seeing them as good. Shared feelings, loyalty, trust, and other interpersonal qualities are more important than individual interests or larger social concerns.

Following the Golden Rule and meeting the expectations of others are the moral themes, at least for immediate relationships.

While these are certainly laudable standards, people stuck in this level are often blind to larger issues. Their need for approval makes them prime targets for others who may use or abuse them. Their exclusive focus on being good and helpful in their relationships can be destructive and ultimately irresponsible.

Level 4: What If Everybody Did It?

These people are acutely aware that individuals can survive together only if they follow certain social rules and laws. Individual needs and relationships must at times give way to larger social agreements and duties. The overriding moral theme is that society or the particular institution would fall apart if everyone pursued his or her own interests.

The risk for people reasoning exclusively from this level is that their sense of duty and commitment to the group will squelch individual rights. Since they take the point of view of the system, they may turn off empathy and rationalize hurtful but necessary behavior. Their concern for the larger good may be admirable, but without some larger guiding principles, it can be very dangerous.

Level 5: There Are Universal Rights and Principles That Should Apply to Everyone

People reasoning from this perspective are aware of all the arguments made by those in level 4, but they take a more independent stance. Their ideas of right and wrong are based on universal principles of justice, equality of human rights, and respect for individual human beings, regardless of the social system or institution. They will challenge and attempt to change laws and social agreements that are not based on valid principles and basic human rights. Since they are aware of the many sides of a moral argument, drawing the line can be a very difficult process.

Individuals immersed exclusively in this level run the risk of becoming too idealistic and intellectual. In addition, they may have great concern for the welfare of many people while overlooking intimacy and caring in their own lives. A balanced dose of level 3 reasoning (putting shared feelings and close relationships above larger social concerns) can be helpful.

USING YOUR BEST JUDGMENT

Knowing the general level of moral reasoning that you use regularly or apply to a particular situation is helpful, but it doesn't necessarily make your decisions easier. Consider the following situation:

Elaine is thirty-two years old, divorced, and the sole provider for Sam, her twelve-year-old son. For the past ten years she has worked as a billing administrator for a private medical clinic specializing in dermatology and plastic surgery. Besides enriching the skillful physicians, the thriving clinic provides an above-average livelihood for the supporting staff. Dr. White, the sixty-four-year-old founder of the clinic, believes that loyalty, commitment, and competence should be sustained and rewarded with top salaries and bonuses. Elaine and her son have benefited greatly by his generosity. The clinic has been like a close-knit family for most employees.

Although somewhat intimidated by Dr. White's firm, authoritarian manner, Elaine is very much taken with his sense of compassion and humanity. In fact, he reminds her of her own father, who died of heart failure shortly after her divorce.

Six months ago, Dr. White dramatically increased the flow of patients by hiring four nonmedical cosmetologists and training them to administer a special facial treatment he has developed. A stimulating facial massage and a deep-cleansing mask are followed by an application of antioxidants, collagen, and other secret ingredients. After seeing one of the physicians for an initial evaluation, satisfied patients have come back week after week to invigorate aging skin. Most rave about the $100 treatments, particularly since they don't pay a dime. Their insurance companies pick up the tab. Everyone is happy, except Elaine.

This is Elaine's dilemma. Although she has been told to bill the treatments as medically necessary for damaged skin or facial rashes, she has learned that most of the patients use the treatments cosmetically, as a hedge against aging. The treatments aren't medically necessary as generally defined by the insurance companies. According to her own observations, the facial rashes described in the medical records are often nonexistent or exaggerated. Furthermore, she has discovered that the cosmetologists alone are administering the procedure and, after the initial exam, are infrequently supervised by the physicians. Technically, the billings could be seen as fraudulent. Even worse, what if harmful side effects should not be detected by the cosmetologists? After all, some of the secret ingredients have not been formally tested. What if they're absorbed into the blood or something?

Elaine has grown increasingly concerned and shocked that Dr. White would condone such a practice. She knows him as honest and well-meaning, with his patients' interests foremost in mind. Like many dedicated physicians, he often goes to extremes to meet his patients' needs, even if it means circumventing the bureaucracy. But this time he may have gone too far, for their needs or his own. Elaine does not know whose needs are taking precedence here.

When she gently approaches Dr. White about the matter, he laughs it off and says she's thinking too much like a nitpicking lawyer. "Besides," he says, "patients should have access to available treatments. We can't let the insurance companies decide these things. We're preventing premature aging, enhancing self-image, and increasing the patient's sense of well-being. This in turn leads to better health. How can the insurance companies complain about that? These treatments are perfectly safe and cost-effective."

What should she do? Her commitment to Dr. White and the clinic runs deep, but this may be over the line. She could be held liable or even criminally culpable if this comes to light. Should she quit and lose the best job she's ever had? Or perhaps she's already in too deep. Should she blow the whistle to protect herself? But what would happen to her friends, the other employees? They might end up hating her. After all, they are doing very well and don't seem to care about the situation. And what about the larger implications? If she does nothing, isn't that tantamount to ripping off everyone who gets stuck with extraordinary insurance premiums? Even worse, what about the welfare of present and future patients? What if there are unpredictable side effects in the long run? Elaine considers herself a good person, but that perception is now at risk.

Since other people will be affected by her actions, Elaine faces the difficult task of determining the moral thing to do based on her personal standards and the universal moral values. At this point, she must try to find a solution that best approximates a moral ideal, even though she may ultimately decide to follow another course of action. For a final decision, her own feelings, needs, and personal values will have to be weighed and juggled in the equation. (As you know, people aren't always able or willing to follow an ideal, even though they may see it.)

Elaine feels terribly alone and emotionally drained. She has a special affection for Dr. White, which complicates her dilemma. Since the death of her father and the end of her marriage, she has looked to Dr. White as a formidable father-figure as well as a boss. Forcefully confronting and opposing him would be quite difficult and painful. In search of other perspectives, she poses the dilemma to her support group, which she has attended since her father's death. The range of feedback she receives is quite surprising. Each response seems to reflect a certain level of moral reasoning, the criterion each member uses for deciding right and wrong in this particular situation.

Desmond: "Don't mess with a good thing. It's really not clear if your boss is doing anything illegal. Even if he is, the chances of you getting in trouble are nil. Who's going to blame you? You're not diagnosing and treating anyone." (Desmond's reasoning for right and wrong, in this instance, appears to lie in level 1, It's Right If You Don't Get in Trouble.)

Anthony: "You have to look out for Number One, but you really owe your boss for hiring you in the first place, giving you a decent living. Sure, he's probably gone over the line—but you owe him. And you might need his cooperation in the future for something else. Look the other way." (Anthony bases his decision on level 2, Protect Your Own Self-Interest.)

Valerie: "If you don't go along, you'll be hurting yourself, your son, and all of your friends at the clinic. Their families would also be affected. Do you really want to be responsible for upsetting their lives like this? And for what? You'd hate yourself. You've got to trust Dr. White like you always have." (Valerie appears to be guided by level 3, Your Personal Relationships Are Everything.)

Patrick: "In my opinion, it's very clear. The billing is fraudulent. I'd threaten to blow the whistle. What if every clinic stretched the rules like this? We'd all go broke paying our insurance premiums. Furthermore, Dr. White's treatment has not been tested in controlled situations. There are regulations about these things." (Patrick's perspective lies somewhere in level 4, What If Everybody Did It?)

Jane: "I agree with Patrick but there's even more at stake here. Rules or not, it's simply not fair to make the rest of us pay for someone else's vanity. Nor is it fair to the patients, who are not being closely monitored by the doctors. They could be at risk. Plus, the physicians are routinely lying in the medical records. That's not right. How can you justify lying to temporarily smooth away a few wrinkles?" (Jane appears to have strong elements of level 5 reasoning, There Are Universal Rights and Principles That Should Apply to Everyone, in her argument.)

There is truth underlying all of the members' suggestions, but Elaine doesn't necessarily agree with their conclusions. Basically, she concurs with Jane's reasoning the most, even though she feels emotionally overwhelmed by the thought of violating loyalty to Dr. White and hurting other employees. For her, the strongest pulls are coming from level 3, Your Relationships Are Everything, and level 5, There Are Universal Rights and Principles That Should Apply to Everyone. After careful consideration, Elaine decides that confronting her boss and refusing to go along with the treatments and the billing policy seems like the morally ideal thing to do. But there are many complications—other things to consider, feelings to work through, and values to balance.

MAKING THE DIFFICULT DECISION

In the real world, Elaine can't simply search for "the right answer." She must use her best judgment to make a very difficult, *responsible* choice. How is she going to do it? Here are some general guidelines that can clarify the situation and identify what's at stake. Several of the steps have been adapted from the work of Kent Hodgson, Ph.D. His enlightening book, *A Rock and a Hard Place* (AMACOM, 1992), is geared toward ethical decision-making in business, but the general principles are valuable in daily life. This approach stresses personal responsibility as well as cooperation.

BENCHMARK NO. 9

SEVEN STEPS FOR
MAKING DIFFICULT MORAL DECISIONS

1. **Gather the facts.**   At this stage, your goal is to get all the facts, while suspending judgment. What's the situation? How did it appear to happen? Who's involved?

2. **Determine whether you have any negative feelings toward any of the people involved.**   Negative feelings and ill intentions can cloud your judgment. Look at your own motivations. Be aware of possible biases.

3. **Identify *what* each person wants to do, *how* he or she wants to do it, and *why*.**   Identify all the practical reasons that people might give for their position, as well as the means they choose to achieve their ends. Include yourself here. Suspend judgment.

4. **For each approach, try to project the possible outcomes.**   How severe are the consequences to the people involved? What are the larger implications? Who might get hurt and how much?

5. **Try to place yourself in each person's shoes.**   Ask yourself two questions: "If I were in your place, how would I be feeling and thinking?" and "If I were in your place, how would I like to be treated, and what would I expect of the other people involved?" This can help clarify issues of fairness.

6. **Identify the universal moral values behind each outcome and action.**   Do any of the possible *ends* (outcomes) violate your personal standards or universal values? Do any *means* (actions) used to

achieve those ends violate those standards? Which values seem to be given priority in each position (e.g., fairness, caring, respect, responsibility, honesty, loyalty, liberty)? Applied to whom (self, immediate family, business, community, society at large)?

7. **Decide which values are the most responsible and important for you in this particular situation. Choose an action that best reflects those values.** This is the hardest step. Your decision will be highly personal but based on sound principles. You have carefully considered viewpoints, actions, possible outcomes, and values to the best of your ability. Others may disagree, but you will be able to defend *your* principled choices. That's the *best* that anyone can do.

Of course, not all moral decisions require a heavy-duty process like this. More often than not, we're likely to make our daily decisions very quickly and intuitively, without resorting to a series of complicated steps. However, there are times when we face true dilemmas, when all sides may have significant merit. That's when we need to give our reasoning and feeling process some structure. Let's see how these steps work for Elaine. Although difficult at first, they become easier and more automatic with practice. Keep in mind that Elaine's conclusions are not necessarily right. You and I, in our own process of moral discovery, might come up with something quite different.

Step 1: Gather the Facts

At this point, Elaine suspends her judgment and collects as much information as possible. Here's the situation as she sees it:

Our clinic has a fine reputation and we've all been proud to work there. We're paid very well and enjoy the familylike atmosphere. Since Dr. White developed his new facial treatment, business has been booming. The problem is, for billing purposes, we're saying that the treatments are for facial rashes and other skin problems, rather than for normal aging. To cover the diagnosis, the skin problems are exaggerated in the patients' charts. Also, the treatments involve experimental ingredients and I'm afraid they aren't being monitored closely enough by the physicians. Something could go wrong; patients could get hurt.

When I question Dr. White, he doesn't take my concerns seriously. He feels he's doing the right thing by giving his patients what they want. He swears the treatments are safe and won't say much more about it. The problem is, with no debate on the issue, he's asking me to lie. As the billing administrator, I have a responsibility in this. But where do I draw the line? Clinics have always circumvented the insurance bureaucracy when necessary. But are fancy facials really necessary? And are they safe?

Step 2: Determine Negative Feelings Toward the People Involved

Dr. White. I admire Dr. White and have always looked up to him. His respect and approval are very important to me. I'm afraid of losing his friendship. He's been like a second father to me. But, like that of my own father, his manner has always been intimidating and somewhat rigid. Sometimes I feel like striking out at him, putting him in his place. I grew up with the same feelings, even though I loved my father very much. Do I want to challenge Dr. White for my own ego, my own sense of power? Like a father-daughter thing? I don't think that's my motivation here. It's more likely that I'd overlook something wrong to please him.

I'm not sure that I can always trust Dr. White's judgment. He can be blinded by his own pursuits. This isn't the first time that he has convinced himself that something was right. Several years ago he got caught up in the early liposuction craze and began pushing the procedure before other alternatives were adequately considered. His enthusiasm can overwhelm his better judgment.

Step 3: Identify What Each Person Wants to Do, *How* He or She Wants to Do It, and *Why*

Dr. White. He wants to give patients what makes them happy and enhances their lives, and he wants to refine his new treatment. He also wants to make money. I know that's important to him but it's probably not his primary motivation. He says, "Who is to determine what is necessary for each patient? Do we really want the insurance companies dictating these things? For some people, wrinkled, prematurely aging facial features can be more debilitating than eczema on the chest. Why should insurance pay for one and not the other? They're both skin problems that can benefit from treatment. We can't reserve these revolutionary treatments for the wealthy. Not everyone can pay out of pocket."

To accomplish these ends, he wants his physicians to exaggerate the medical reasons for the facial treatments. He also wants me to submit questionable insurance billing.

Other Employees at the Clinic. They're a tightly knit group, people my boss has handpicked and nurtured over the years. They want to be good, loyal employees and do what's best for the clinic and the patients without sacrificing their integrity. From what I hear, most are following Dr. White's lead. The general consensus seems to be: "We're providing a great service and no one is complaining. The treatment is safe and effective, truly a breakthrough in dermatology. And, like most clinics, we've always done battle with insurance companies, so this is nothing new."

Myself. I want to be fair about this and do what's best, without hurting anyone. But I'm not sure that's possible. One thing is for certain: I would feel absolutely terrible and ashamed if we're ever investigated. With the health care crisis, all sorts of regulatory agencies are cracking down on questionable practices. And if someone is really hurt by the treatments, I'd be devastated. I don't want to be a part of this whole thing

What should I do? One option would be to confront Dr. White, tell him about my reservations, and threaten to quit. I could simply walk away if he doesn't agree. Or I could threaten to blow the whistle unless some changes are made. In the long run, this might be better for the clinic, get it back on track. Or I could do nothing, keep quiet, earn a good living. Business as usual.

Step 4: For Each Approach or Option, Project the Possible Outcomes

Dr. White's Approach. On the positive side, he is helping his patients, refining a potentially important new treatment, and increasing the prestige of the clinic. We've all been given considerable bonuses for our extra efforts, and the patients are happy.

On the negative side, this can't go on forever. Someone or some computer will pick up on the dramatic increase in billing for these treatments. The balloon will burst and we'll all be in trouble. Even if it doesn't come to light, it still feels as if we're doing something wrong, taking advantage, and maybe putting patients at risk. It just doesn't feel right. We're contributing to a national problem.

My Options

Option No. 1: Confront my boss, threaten to quit. On the positive side, I would retain my self-respect, stand up for what I feel and believe, and possibly get him to change his mind. My actions might protect the clinic in the long run. On the negative side, he'd be upset but would probably just let me go. Then my life and my son's life would be a real mess. Good jobs are hard to come by around here. We'd probably have to move.

Option No. 2: Threaten to blow the whistle if things don't change. On the positive side, I'd get Dr. White to face reality, possibly make some changes. I'm convinced his present course is putting everyone in jeopardy. Maybe I wouldn't be able to actually go through with it but it might be worth the threat. On the negative side, such a threat or action would forever change his feelings about me. I'd also lose most of my friends at the clinic. A major price to pay.

Option No. 3. Forget about the whole thing, cover my tail the best I can. At some point everyone may come to his of her senses about this, before it blows. If I have patience, the whole conflict might be avoided. I'd keep my job and life would go on. And it's not as if people are really being hurt. The financial thing is a drop in the bucket compared to most medical procedures, and none of the patients has reported any side effects thus far. On the negative side, how would I feel about myself if I continue to look the other way?

Step 5: Place Yourself in Each Person's Shoes

Dr. White's Shoes. If I were in his shoes, I would be very excited about the positive results of my new treatment and would want to try it on anyone who was interested. I'd be thinking about the greater good that might come from the availability of my treatment, as well as my own prestige. I'd also enjoy the increase in income. In his place, I would want to be treated with respect and loyalty by my staff. I would want others to value and trust my judgment. However, unlike Dr. White, I would be more open to other opinions. He didn't even ask me what I thought or felt about this matter. That is not fair.

Our Patients. I'd be ecstatic that I found something that made me look and feel better. Since the cosmetologists are administering it, I'd probably assume that it's perfectly safe, like a regular facial. However, if something went wrong, like a hard-to-detect internal reaction, I'd feel really betrayed. And I wouldn't be at all happy that the evaluations are being exaggerated in my medical record. As things stand now, patients aren't even aware that this is happening.

The General Public. If I weren't involved in this, I'd be outraged and would probably see it as another scam by a group of greedy physicians. Just another symptom of a medical system gone crazy. With all the talk about accountability and managed care, I'd wonder why the insurance companies didn't monitor the billing better. I'd also wonder why none of the clinic employees spoke up.

Step 6: Identify the Universal Moral Values Behind Each Outcome and Action

It's likely that Dr. White and I will give different weights to the values involved. *We'll apply them according to what we care about the most.* In reality, I don't know what values he thinks he is following or how he might define them. But I have to use my best judgment to assess what's involved here. He may not agree.

My boss wants to help people, enhance his prestige, and expand the clinic. He is willing to stretch the rules to accomplish this end. I know he values *re-*

sponsibility but perhaps this is limited to his immediate world—the clinic and his patients, at least in this instance. He *cares* about the people who surround him and feels responsible for their welfare, but in my opinion, he places all of us at risk. Plus, he doesn't extend the Golden Rule to the public at large. They would probably be outraged by $100 cosmetic facials added to the swollen medical system, as well as the falsified records. *Loyalty* is extremely important to my boss. He values *liberty* and freedom of choice, particularly when it comes to treatment options. He sees the insurance company's definition of "medical necessity" as too restrictive and feels that it overlooks the holistic, cost-effective value of certain treatments.

I agree in principle with the positive outcome that he is trying to achieve. But the means he's using are not acceptable to me. Larger issues are at stake, like *honesty*. Plus, we have a *responsibility* to ethical medical practice in general to play by agreed-upon guidelines. We can't change the general ground rules every time they conflict with something we'd like to do.

Furthermore, I don't think my boss is being *fair, respectful,* or *responsible* to me by leaving me out of the decision-making process regarding the billing procedures. I wouldn't have treated him like that. He just expects me and everyone else to go along, without any debate. I'm surprised the other physicians haven't objected.

What about the values behind my own options? If I confront my boss and threaten to quit or blow the whistle, I'd be stressing *honesty,* for my own conscience and integrity; respect, for myself and the public at large; and *responsibility,* for ethical practice in general. However, in the minds of the other employees I would be violating loyalty to the clinic and treating everyone unfairly. And I might gain nothing other than a clear conscience. How important is that to me?

If I go along with everything, I'd be following and/or neglecting the same values as my boss. I'm not sure I could do that.

Step 7: Decide Which Values Are the Most Important and Responsible for You in This Situation

I want to help patients and the clinic just like my boss does. But I don't like the way he plans to do it. Also, maybe I have a wider perspective on this. His level of moral reasoning, at least in this situation, doesn't seem to extend to level 4 or 5 (What If Everybody Did It? and There Are Universal Rights and Principles That Should Apply to Everyone). He'd probably argue with this, saying that unfair rules must be challenged and that he is working for the greater good. I think he's rationalizing his own agenda.

When I look at all the values involved, the ones I value the most seem to point me in one direction: Tell Dr. White that I can't go along with this, that I would have trouble respecting myself if I did. Maybe we can come up with another solution. Maybe not. Maybe I'll have to resign or blow the whistle. I can't know all the consequences now, but this is the best I can do. This whole thing could blow up in my face, in ways that I can't know or predict. Maybe I'm overlooking or misjudging something, but it doesn't seem so now. Although others may not accept it, it feels as if I'm making the best, principled decision that I can. I hope I have the courage to follow through with it. [In the next chapter, we will see if Elaine actually does what she intends.]

FLIES IN THE OINTMENT

The path that Elaine has chosen is very near the general moral ideal she had determined from the very beginning:

"This whole thing is dishonest. Patients might be at risk, and we're taking advantage of the system and everyone who must pay for it." Her decision seems to follow her gut-level response, even though she used reasoning to sort through all the values and alternatives. She has given the situation careful thought, examined her own feelings and motives, and tried to be objective.

But a moral ideal is not always followed by Elaine, or anyone else. Sometimes our chosen path is miles from our moral ideal—if we have an ideal at all. Sometimes the ideal is, in fact, unreachable. Nothing is perfect. Life is full of painful choices and compromises. Sometimes we're absolutely convinced that our path is based on principles, when in reality it's being twisted by other motives. People will be people.

As you have seen in previous chapters, our decisions are often influenced by skewed perceptions, selective blindness, excuses, and psychological defenses. The other characters in our moral theater have not been immune to these limitations. Let's see how their paths are shaping up.

Jennifer. You might think that Jennifer's moral dilemma is related to her criminal activities: violating the rights and property of innocent people and the use of violence to settle arguments. Unfortunately, in her eyes, that's not the case. Although she sometimes experiences pangs of guilt when alone, her empathy remains in cold storage.

Jennifer's dilemma centers on Scott, her twenty-year-old boyfriend. (See page 41 for the beginning of her story.) Although she hasn't seen him in weeks, she still *feels* when she thinks of him—love, passion, empathy, concern, respect, all the positive emotions that have been diminished in recent years. She cares enough to sense any dilemmas about Scott, to consider his perspectives and needs.

But where is Scott? Since the pregnancy, he has made no effort to contact her. As the weeks go by without the usual letters and secret late-night phone calls, the hurt builds. For the first time, she's frightened of her future as a single parent. As the reality sets in, Jennifer's fear and hurt give way to one of the emotions she knows best—anger.

She wants to hurt Scott and protect him at the same time. While her hope is fading, her love still feels strong. She wonders if it's right to betray him, to threaten something vengeful, like tipping off the police. Will he pay attention then?

When a friend reluctantly tells Jennifer that Scott has moved in with a nineteen-year-old woman, the dilemma is resolved. To her grandmother's surprise, Jennifer says she will file charges of statutory rape. She tells Nanna, "It's the right thing to do. I'm not going to be one of those women who sit back and get taken for a ride by some guy. He has a responsibility here."

While her decision may indeed be right and just, the process that led to this decision was based on hurt, fear, and anger rather than any principles or values. Her real agenda is clouded by the moral high ground that she now claims.

Zachary. Zachary is the sophisticated con man who bilked thousands of senior citizens. He formed a phony foundation and lined his pockets with contributions. (See page 40 for his story.) He was raised by authoritarian parents who tried to instill values by lecturing and imposing strict rules. He never really bonded emotionally with his parents but was able to mouth their values like a sophisticated parrot. At present, he is facing his second charge of mail fraud. The only dilemma that Zachary sees is getting caught. He's firmly entrenched in level 1 moral reasoning: It's Right If You Don't Get in Trouble.

He claims that the government unfairly used entrapment. "It was a setup, plain and simple. What they did was illegal. They had no right." In his case, legal maneuvering and technicalities may circumvent larger values. Zachary's judicial rights are pitted against the rights of his victims.

Vanessa. Unfortunately, at this time, Vanessa is stuck in a codependent relationship and fails to see any dilemma other than "How am I going to get Eric to stop hitting me without destroying our relationship?" She's capable of seeing many levels of a moral dilemma, but in this particular situation, she is blind. Her thinking here does not go beyond level 3 moral reasoning—Your Personal Relationships Are Everything. Even so, she's overlooking the welfare of her son. Her husband, Eric, sees a relationship problem but no moral dilemma.

Richard. Richard, you may remember from Part I of this book, is the nineteen-year-old son of David, the attorney having an affair with his legal assistant. (David's story begins on page 12.) Richard attends a prestigious engineering school and is faced with the moral dilemma of whether to cheat on a major exam. If he doesn't cheat, he could fail. If he cheats and gets caught, he could be expelled. His thinking goes something like this:

> Cheating is wrong. I know I shouldn't do it. I should be able to pass the course fairly. But is anything fair in life? Politicians cheat and lie, corporate executives cover up.... I bet the professor has cheated sometimes to get where he is. The world is hypocritical. Why should I be ethical about this and get left in the dust? Since everyone else in the class seems to be cheating, the odds would be against me. It's not fair. I really don't feel guilty about this. It's necessary. I'm going to do it.

Richard does have a moral ideal, but he's overwhelmed by group pressure and the stress of the moment. He has taken on the dog-eat-dog mentality that characterizes levels 1 and 2 in moral reasoning, even though he's capable of a much broader perspective. Somehow, he's convinced himself that the situation is unfair—so cheating is the only fair thing to do.

If Richard gave it more thought, perhaps he would see that cheating: (1) violates trust between the teacher and the students; (2) misrepresents knowledge and ability; (3) penalizes those who choose not to cheat; (4) snowballs into other lies and deceptions; and (5) undermines self-respect.

David.   David, Richard's father, knows without a doubt that his torrid affair with Shana, is violating every standard that he believes in. His problem has very little to do with his capacity for moral reasoning. The guilt and shame are killing him. Yet he feels hopelessly mired, sucked in by conflicting needs, romantic impulses, and vague obligations to Shana. Shana, you may remember, has many personality problems, and tends to hold on to love and attention with manipulation and veiled threats. David wishes he could rid himself of dangerous yearnings for her, turn back the clock, and rebuild his relationship with Noreen, his wife of twenty years. But the die has been cast. He must accept responsibility for what has happened and make some decisions.

He knows it can't go on. The problem is, every alternative, every way out is fraught with destructive consequences. Shana is an explosive powder keg, primed to hurl shrapnel in all directions. Her veiled threats leave no doubt in his mind that she would call Noreen, file suit for sexual harassment, attack him physically, or seriously harm herself. Her finely laid web of trip wires is complete and paralyzing.

Leaving Shana would mean hurting or indirectly killing her, a lawsuit, the loss of his job, or the possible demise of his marriage. And there's no guarantee that Noreen, the person that he truly loves, would be willing or able to move beyond the terrible pain he has inflicted upon her. He even thought about leaving Noreen to free her of this mess.

Staying with Shana would be impossible. She's incapable of sustaining a relationship. Sooner or later, she would turn on him and extract whatever she could from the ashes of their liason. He could wait until she rejected him, but the inevitable results would only be delayed.

David knows the right thing to do, without going through a complex reasoning process. Everyone will pay the price for his breach of trust, in ways that he may never know. But the time has come to face the consequences. If only he could do it.

Shana. David's lover has learned to deal with the world through manipulation and threats. (For the story of her unfortunate childhood, including incest and emotional neglect, see page 62.) In spite of her apparent treachery, she is deeply hurt by the emptiness in her life and plagued by a relentless fear of abandonment. Quite literally, she's hanging on by a thread, a thread that leads to David. Her desperate *need* for him feels "as if" she loves him. Her confusion in this regard is very real.

For Shana, doing the right thing means doing anything to secure her well-being and drive away painful feelings. She has a larger perspective of right and wrong but only in an abstract, ideal sense. When she is hurting, which is most of the time, she's unable to sort through the complex factors behind most moral dilemmas. Her point of view is bound by her pain and her narcissism. More often than not, she feels morally justified and superior in her revenge.

Shana is convinced that David, like everyone else, will reject her. In fact, she purposely mistreats him to drive him away, then makes amends in fear of losing him. In her mind, she's already devised a plan for the inevitable end. She will hate him with a vengeance. He will be evil, malicious, contemptuous—a moral degenerate. She will destroy him and show the world how she has suffered at his abusive hands. He violated his responsibility as her boss, and now he must pay. It's the right thing to do.

Noreen. David's forty-five-year-old wife knows nothing of his affair but is drowning in self-doubt and apprehension. Her very rewarding, loving marriage of twenty years is disintegrating. David is a zombie, going through the motions, freezing her out, while reassuring her at the same time. His words sound sincere, but his eyes are empty and elusive. Their intense conversations feel destructive and circular, like a snake devouring its own tail.

Even worse, David is seldom home anymore. Noreen spends her time waiting, crying, distracting herself with work. But nothing changes. Something has to happen—a separation, a divorce, anything to dissolve the wretched uncertainty.

Perhaps he doesn't love her anymore. Perhaps he's clinically depressed, in a midlife crisis. Perhaps he's seeing someone else. Until now, the second possibility was all that Noreen would allow herself to consider. But something must be done. She can't make a decision about a separation or divorce without more information. And David talks in circles. For now, this is the crux of her moral dilemma: Should she spy on the man who has never intentionally hurt her, the man whom she has trusted explicitly for twenty years?

Noreen goes through as many of the possible outcomes as she can imagine—finding him with someone else, finding nothing but getting caught by David in the process, finding nothing but feeling ashamed for her betrayal of his trust, and so forth. Placing herself in his shoes, she wouldn't want to be spied on like this, but she would understand and forgive the insecurity driving the breach of trust. Perhaps David would understand that it's a symptom of larger problems. Maybe it would bring things to a head. Noreen does not believe that it's the right thing to do. She believes it is necessary.

Intentions Are Not Actions

It's one thing to make a moral decision and come up with a plan of action; it's another matter entirely to actually carry it out. While powers of moral reasoning, personal standards, and conscience can lead the way, a host of personal failings can thwart the best, or worst, of intentions. We're entering another realm here—stamina, commitment, competence, self-control, willpower—qualities of character that breathe life into moral ideals. We need to take a closer look at the powers that make our intentions real. Sometimes they desert us, lead us astray, or never materialize in the first place.

TEN

Walking the Line: Following Your Best Judgment . . . and More

Remember Elaine, the billing administrator at the private medical clinic? We ran through her moral dilemma in the previous chapter. Elaine is quite upset because Dr. White, the sixty-four-year-old founder and chief physician, is asking her to submit questionable billings to insurance companies. He has developed a special facial treatment administered by cosmetologists to counter the effects of natural aging. But in order for the insurance companies to pay for the treatments, they must be deemed medically necessary rather than simply cosmetic. To this end, Dr. White and his colleagues are exaggerating their evaluations and diagnoses to justify the facials. Furthermore, in Elaine's opinion, the physicians are lax in their monitoring of the experimental treatments. Side effects could go undetected, placing patients at risk.

Although Elaine was immediately concerned about the ethical implications, she was caught in a dilemma. Her future and her son's, and the well-being of the other clinic employees, could be jeopardized if she opposed Dr. White or interfered with his plans. But after thinking it through, she decided that she couldn't condone the billing practice or the treatments, regardless of the personal consequences. Now it is time to confront her boss.

Elaine is extremely apprehensive about approaching Dr. White. In many ways, he reminds her of her own late father and triggers all the conflicts of love, power, authority, and autonomy often found in father-child relationships. She wants to speak her mind but is fearful of losing his respect and approval at the same time. After her father's sudden death, she has been particularly vulnerable in this area. Dr. White helped fill the void. How is she ever going to confront him, explain her view of the moral dilemma, and threaten to quit or blow the whistle if he disagrees?

She is absolutely disgusted with herself. How can a thirty-two-year-old woman, with many strengths and accomplishments, dissolve so easily? What buttons are being pushed? And what about him? Does her boss have any moral principles beyond responsibility and loyalty to his patients and clinic? Is he of narrow vision, as she tends to see him now, or is he the formidable but caring person who used to talk about honesty, fairness, and larger principles?

Elaine's inner turmoil takes its toll when she finally meets him alone. She is shaking inside, the mature woman hampered by scripts from the past. He is comforting and gracious, assuring her that her concerns are well-taken. He too is worried about the potential of an insurance investigation but feels that the gains made by his new treatment far outweigh the risks. "You've seen the results. They're absolutely remarkable. Don't you think we have an obligation to further refine the treatments and develop them for the public at large? Our clinic is the perfect setting for this, without the interference and bureaucracy found at research hospitals. We can make a difference, even if we have to fudge things a little as we go along. The special emollients are derived from rain forest plants found only in Costa Rica. They're very expensive. We're actually losing money on the deal.

"As far as we know, the treatments are no more risky than scores of over-the-counter facial conditioners. In six months, we've had only half a dozen adverse reactions, all of which disappeared when the concentrations were adjusted. The emollients are safe enough for a baby's bottom. Would you be worried about rubbing vitamins, collagen, and special herbs on your face? Of course not. If your skin became irritated or something, you'd simply stop. Furthermore, each patient signs a consent form that lists all conceivable side effects. We're not hiding anything here."

Elaine loses her thoughts in the sincere flow of his words and is unable to respond. His perspective seems to make sense, but she has a nagging feeling in her heart. How does he know that the rain forest ingredients aren't being absorbed into the body in some way? They're new and experimental, so who knows? What about blood tests and more thorough monitoring? Not wanting to challenge Dr. White's authority, she lets the question pass. But why hadn't he discussed all of this with her before? He informs her that he did not want to put her on the spot, that he wanted to take full responsibility for the insurance billings and the consequences.

As a final gesture, he writes up and signs a summary of their meeting, listing Elaine's concerns and his responses. "If we get audited or in trouble in some way, this should help get you off the hook. But really, you're making far too much of this. I can legitimately justify everything we're doing. You'll be proud to be a part of our breakthrough."

Elaine is completely disarmed. Over the next several days, she is in absolute turmoil. Maybe Dr. White is right, maybe she has blown this thing all out of proportion. He has always been a good man, with high standards. She has never, ever questioned his intentions. Why shouldn't she trust his seasoned judgment? Maybe she's just being too cautious, emotional. She eventually decides, with great relief, that she has overreacted to the whole thing. *Everything will be all right. My job, my son's security, my friends, the patients.* Dr. White will see to it.

PITFALLS

Elaine is backpedaling and deceiving herself, not about whether her boss is right or wrong, but about her own feelings. Dr. White's perspective is compelling and might be supported by a vast array of knowledgeable, well-meaning people. But in her heart, and still in the back of her mind, Elaine feels and believes her original position: *It's not right that the doctors are lying in the charts, that I am being asked to sub-*

mit trumped-up bills, that patients may be placed at risk.
But at the moment, she is overriding these concerns and rationalizing her lapse of willpower.

This is not at all unusual when people must actually walk the line they have chosen. After determining the right thing to do or even earlier, *we may consciously or subconsciously decide that the cost is too high. We may fool ourselves into believing that our original good judgment about the situation was in error.*

Backpedaling is just one of the many pitfalls that challenge good character and thwart our best intentions. Other potential traps include laziness, anxiety, a fear of looking foolish, a bad or hopeless mood, and fatigue. Under those circumstances, it's easy to lose sight of our goal, fall into more pleasant distractions, or opt for less stressful alternatives.

Overcoming obstacles like these requires stamina, competence, perseverance, self-control, willpower, and a host of other personal qualities. Carrying out good, principled intentions can be a great test of character, a test that we all fail at times. As we have seen with Elaine, the emotional price may exceed our available personal strength or our willingness to change.

QUALITIES AND QUIRKS OF CHARACTER

Character lies at the heart of our moral being, our moral personality. It's more than just a strong personality. Adolf Hitler had a strong personality and accomplished many of his malicious goals, yet few people would say that he was a man of character. Character includes all the personal virtues that we might aspire to—self-discipline, courage, integrity, and so forth—as well as the universal principles and values that we choose to place in action. Character fuels our ability to make moral decisions, walk the line, and avoid the pitfalls.

What can we conclude about Elaine's character? In spite of her lapse here, you would probably agree that she is basically a good person, a person of character. But at the moment, in this particular situation at her clinic, you might not think that she is behaving as if she has good character. She has fallen into the role of the dutiful employee, subordinating her better judgment to the will of other people.

If her clinic is investigated for fraudulent billing practices, her character will be questioned. And yet, in almost every sphere of her life, she has been courageous and ethical. Unfortunately, her present dilemma happens to encroach upon and activate some of her deepest fears and vulnerabilities regarding loss, love, and security. Her father's death remains an unhealed scar protected by Dr. White. Although this is no excuse, her psychological defenses have kicked in to partially cover her feelings in this regard.

Elaine is still a good person, but she will have to come to grips with the vulnerabilities—the need for approval, the child/adult nature of her relationship with Dr. White, the continuing grief over her father—that have put some chinks in her good character. Ultimately, her painful experiences could be enlightening. The moral boot camp often leads to a renewed sense of personal strength, meaning, and purpose.

In fact, this is exactly what happened to Elaine. In her own words, here's how her dilemma evolved:

> Everything seemed okay for a couple of weeks after I met with Dr. White. Then I started feeling really guilty about it again and had a dream that my father was watching everything I did at the clinic, shaking his head. He was a stickler for honesty but he didn't trust many people at all, particularly accountants, lawyers, and doctors. In fact, getting him to see any professional was like pulling teeth.
>
> The truth is, he died because he refused to get his blood cholesterol and his heart functioning checked. He had symptoms for years but ignored them. "The doctors just make everything worse. They did nothing for your mother, now did they? She suffered more at their hands than without them." I gave up trying to

convince him otherwise. He was always pigheaded
and lost trust in doctors after my mother died. And
he certainly didn't value the judgment of his grown
up "little girl."

Then it really hit me. My father may have died
prematurely *because he lost trust in doctors.* And here
I am at the clinic, cranking out reams of trumped-up
diagnoses, watching patients come in week after week
getting their face slathered with some weird plant
from the rain forest, telling myself that it's all okay. It's
nuts. I came to this job shortly after my mother died.
In fact, I really wanted to be a physician's assistant,
but I had a two-year-old son. You know how it goes.
Anyway, I really respected doctors. *Trust, respect.*
These things started to hit home again. Dr. White was
a wonderful, dear man, but he was wavering off
course. Somebody had to tell him.

He was shocked. I yelled, I cried, I told him I
couldn't sit by and watch this, in spite of his good intentions. He was putting everyone at risk, including
his patients, because of some pipe dream. I suggested
that if he believes so firmly in his treatment, he
should do it right, set it up as a formal research project at a hospital, put it to a real test, stop all the fudg-
ing, the little lies that add up to mistrust and disre-
spect. Unlike my father, he really listened. I was
totally surprised. It felt as if a lifelong shadow had
been lifted. He actually valued what I had to say.

Several months after we discontinued the facial
treatments, as chance would have it, a major television network did an undercover investigation about
fraudulent billing and diagnoses in dermatology and
several other medical specialties. I shuddered as I
watched. Although we could still pay the price for
past practices, Dr. White is carrying on his research in
conjunction with a teaching hospital. He says he has
immense respect for me that I have strength of char-

acter. This is the first time in years that I've done something other than just a "good job."

What's Good Character All About?

Our intuitive feeling about Elaine's good character was correct. But what do we really mean when we say "good" character? Although people may stress different qualities, traits, and virtues in their definition, good character encompasses nearly all the positive skills and attributes that we have seen throughout this book. Good character is part and parcel of what we think, how we feel, and our ability to put our values into action. Weaknesses in any one of these three areas can and do lead good people to bad deeds.

Thomas Lickona, a psychologist at the State University of New York at Cortland, has devoted his professional career to issues of moral development and character. In his important book, *Educating for Character: How Our Schools Can Teach Respect and Responsibility* (Bantam Books, 1991), he presents a model of character that meshes well with the ideas we have explored thus far. In a nutshell, here's an adapted version of his model. Keep in mind that these are ideals, something a person might aim for. It goes without saying, no one can be perfect in all situations.

BENCHMARK NO. 10

KEYS TO GOOD CHARACTER

MORAL KNOWING

1. **Moral Awareness (Sensitivity):** The ability to see that certain situations have moral implications.

2. **Knowing Moral Values:** Knowledge of the universal moral values, what they mean, and how they can be applied.

3. **Perspective-Taking:** The ability to see the viewpoints of other people, to place oneself in the other person's shoes.

4. **Moral Reasoning:** Understanding why we should be moral and why some actions are morally better than others.

5. **Decision-Making:** The ability to think through a moral problem, figuring out choices and consequences.

6. **Self-knowledge:** Knowing ourselves, our strengths and weaknesses.

MORAL FEELING

1. **Conscience:** Knowing what's right and feeling obligated to do what's right.

2. **Self-Esteem:** Valuing and respecting ourselves, which can lead to respect for others.

3. **Empathy:** The ability to vicariously experience the feelings of another person.

4. **Self-Control:** The ability to control emotions when they might lead to unethical behavior.

5. **Humility:** The ability to see through our pride and self-righteousness, a willingness to correct our failings.

MORAL ACTION

1. **Competence:** The ability to turn our moral thinking and feeling into effective moral action, to apply practical skills and carry out a plan of action.

2. **Will:** Strength and courage to carry out what we think we should do.

3. **Habit:** Doing the right thing—considering the needs of others, striving for fairness, honesty, and so forth—automatically, without having to make a conscious decision.

Using these keys to good character as a guide, we can get a quick thumbnail sketch of our moral meandering and see where we've lost our way in a particular dilemma. To illustrate, let's take another look at the players in our moral theater.

Richard, the nineteen-year-old engineering student on the verge of failing, has decided to cheat on a major exam. His decision to buy a bootlegged copy of the exam stems mainly from a lapse in conscience. He knows what's right and is perfectly capable of reasoning it through, but he's not committed to certain moral values enough to act on them in this situation. He doesn't feel *obligated* to do what he knows is best. Furthermore, his guilt has been absolved since "everyone is doing it."

Richard's father, David, is drowning in his extramarital affair with Shana, his legal assistant, because of a lapse in *self-control*. He could give us endless intellectual discourses about morality, good character, and doing the right thing, but his house of cards gave way to some unexpected vibrations from within. Major gaps in *self-knowledge* left him vulnerable in this situation. Ironically, his perfectionism and overcontrol drove him out of control. At present, he has decided that he must leave Shana, regardless of the consequences. Shortly, we will see if he has the *will* to follow through.

Shana, David's twenty-seven-year-old mistress, has very little continuity or core to her narcissistic personality, so many aspects of her character change like the wind. (For an overview of her personality problems and her incestuous childhood, see page 105.) In spite of religious training as a child, she is grossly inconsistent in nearly all areas of moral *knowing*, *feeling*, and *action*. Her mood will determine the course she takes. When she is good, she can be very, very good; but when she is bad . . . Because of this, she presents a very different picture of herself according to the situation. People who know her only briefly or who have dealt with her in casual, stress-free circumstances may have no reason to question her character. For Shana, interpersonal strife dissolves the moral glue.

For Jennifer, the pregnant fifteen-year-old involved in criminal acts with an older group of friends, the moral maze is circular and feeds on itself. Raised by an alcoholic, largely unavailable mother, Jennifer's moral feeling is diminished by low *self-esteem*, blunted *empathy*, and little *self-knowledge*. Lack of moral feeling, in turn, limits her capacity to recognize dilemmas and make moral *decisions*. This will affect how she relates to others and ultimately how she feels about herself. Presently, her self-esteem has plummeted to new lows as Scott, her twenty-year-old boyfriend, deserts her after the pregnancy. In anger, she has decided to charge him with statutory rape. Her *will* to charge him with rape is based on revenge rather than on moral imperatives. Even so, it could be the right thing to do. Through the grapevine, Jennifer has learned that Scott has fathered two other children. And he always walks.

THE ULTIMATE AND MOST INTIMATE SPARK

Up to this point, you may be aware that I have artificially dismantled our moral lives into discreet parts—small, intimate details of thinking, feeling, and doing. The details, however they may be described or organized, are vitally important. Our powers of reasoning seize on them as building blocks for who we are and how we relate to others. Our ego—our consciousness in action—depends upon the intimate details of self-awareness and rational understanding to make and carry out our daily moral choices.

But that's not the whole picture. We are not two-dimensional schematic diagrams hung in a darkened room. As human beings, we seem to have an innate need to understand, not only the intimacies of ourselves, but our relationship to the world and the universe itself. We want to know who we are, why we're here, where we fit in the scheme of things, and what life is all about. In short, we strive for *meaning*.

Without a larger sense of meaning, our spirit may lack the sustenance to thrive, dream, and grow beyond indifference, emptiness, hopelessness, and selfishness. We may lose a crucial spark for doing the right thing. After all, without meaning, why should we care? Why should we agonize and fight the forces of inertia? Why not do what's easiest?

In the broadest dimension, meaning develops into a deep intuitive sense of what is good, true, and dependable beyond ourselves. Most of us have some conception of this, even if it struggles as a delicate flame, quivering fitfully in our subconscious. Our larger vision, however tentative, illuminates and shapes how we choose to lead our lives and how we relate to the universe. In other words, our *faith*—whether defined in a religious context or not—will have an immense effect on the quality of our moral lives. Faith can strengthen our resolve, allow us to dream and work for larger purposes, and help us care enough to follow our best judgment.

We'll look at the broad picture again in the next chapter. But first, we need to see if the characters in our moral theater actually carried out their intentions. The web of responsibility is vast and many of the consequences are unforeseen and unknowable. But once we are morally aware, we must do our best to predict the impact of our actions. Sometimes, the more we know, the greater is our burden.

ENDINGS AND NEW BEGINNINGS

Jennifer. Jennifer's situation tumbled out of control. Impregnated and then deserted by Scott, Jennifer angrily spread the word: Scott would be charged with statutory rape. Her hope was to punish him, force him to change his ways, draw him back in, reject him, love him, and hate him—a sticky mess of convoluted intentions, each one as strong as the other. To Jennifer, he was still the best and worst of her life. And he was the father of her unborn child.

No one but Jennifer knows what really happened next. According to Jennifer's version, she was staying at her mother's condominium complex for the weekend when Scott appeared below her third-story bedroom window.

My mother had gone to bed and I was just lying there, feeling the little kicks in my stomach, wondering if my baby would look like me or Scott. Would I have to live forever seeing his face in my own flesh and blood? Then I heard the pebbles, the tiny clicks on the window that used to stir everything I wished for. I had waited so long for them again but now it was too late. He had no use for me and wouldn't have come if he hadn't heard about the rape charges. Did he think I was stupid or something?

I held my heart and looked down on the street. It was cold and drizzling but there he was, smiling and waving as if he had just come back from a long trip. God, he was beautiful, but I stared at him the way I'd watch a boring movie, take my mind somewhere else. He was real but I couldn't let him be. He was just a picture, a dark shadow on the street, some guy who used me and ran to another pawn. I don't remember feeling anything when I sneaked down the back stairwell and opened the door.

I don't know why I did it. It just didn't matter if I let him in or not. Nothing seemed to matter. He tried to kiss me in the dark but pulled back when he bumped against my stomach. He acted really surprised, as if he had forgotten. Yeah, right. Without saying anything, I turned and tried to walk up the concrete stairs in front of him. Just before the first landing, he slipped his hands up under my robe and started cupping and squeezing me. I remember telling him to stop but he pulled my robe up over his head and began licking the small of my back. His hair, his whole body, was damp and smelled of sweat and someone else's perfume. I wanted to shout "Stop it, stop it! I love you!" like I do to get my drunken mom off my back, but I hated him too much.

I thought of his new girlfriend, his filthy wet tongue, where it had been, and all the lies. I swung around and smacked him in the side of the head with my elbow as hard as I could. I remember a hollow popping sound, like a cork shooting from a bottle. I'd heard it once before when two guys were fighting. And then I remember falling backward, my legs tangled in Scott's arms.

Mom found us at the foot of the stairs. Scott's head was cracked open and there was blood running between my legs. The baby. The police doctor said Scott died from the fall, from hitting the steel guard rail. He said I didn't kill him. No one said I killed him, even though I know I must have.

Eric and Vanessa. As you may remember, Eric and Vanessa were involved in an abusive relationship that kept feeding on itself. Eric denied responsibility and Vanessa made excuses for him, a pattern well-established by their own parents. (You saw Eric and Vanessa's Values Profile—an assessment of the way each relates to the world in a moral sense—beginning on page 73.) Finally, at the urging of friends, Vanessa eventually sought therapy. Eric saw this as a direct threat to his authority and refused to pay for the therapy sessions. But Vanessa joined a self-help group, which incensed him even more. Although he refrained from hitting her out of fear of being reported, he teetered dangerously on the edge.

Vanessa realized that Eric's better behavior was coming from external controls rather than from any sustained, internal changes. He could easily blow again. She explained the situation to her mother, who agreed to become more involved in the care of their son, Eddie. This allowed Vanessa to return to work part-time as a dental hygienist. Although reluctant to do so, she moved half the money in their joint accounts to an account of her own. With a friend present, she gave Eric an ultimatum: Get help or the marriage is over. Her guilt was immense, particularly when Eric began sobbing and pleading like a little boy. He needed her so much.

Eric attended a specialized therapy group that focused on ways to defuse the anger within, as well as the shame, low self-esteem, and inadequacy that fueled it. He learned to identify *trigger thoughts* that were based on unrealistic expectations, faulty assumptions, mistaken entitlements, blaming, and a host of other self-deceptive games of control. He worked on replacing many of these thoughts with *coping thoughts*. Coping thoughts helped to reframe the way that he perceived stressful situations. When his perceptions were less self-centered, defensive, and controlling, the storm was less likely to brew.

Unfortunately, Eric dropped out when the focus turned to personal issues. He was not willing to look at his own vulnerabilities. Nevertheless, Vanessa continued her own work to reclaim many of the values she had lost, such as integrity, honesty, self-determination, and responsibility as a parent. As her self-respect and confidence grew, her capacity for empathy and caring needed outlets beyond her limited relationship with Eric. Her network of friends expanded and she became involved with community concerns. She felt a renewed sense of meaning and purpose.

Although Eric no longer hit Vanessa, the negative forces that fed the codependent relationship were waning. With only one partner invested in change, the void grew deeper. Eric moved out in disgust and filed for separation. Vanessa lost her bearing several times and yearned to rejoin him. Guilt, empathy for Eric, rose-colored memories, an inability to let go of years of emotional investment, and wishful thinking were powerful enticements.

Predictably, their reconciliations were temporary and empty. Eric began a lengthy, vindictive custody battle over Eddie, who would come to symbolize the power he was losing. Eric vowed to raise his son away from Vanessa's influence, to make him a tenacious *man* of his own mold. The judge saw things differently.

David, Shana, Noreen, and Richard.   As you may remember, David's best intention was to leave Shana, his legal assistant and secret lover, at all costs. The torrid, troubled affair was destroying his life and devouring his guilty soul. Shana, following her usual pattern of emotional entanglement, lack of fulfillment, and subsequent rage, suspected that she would be rejected again and made plans to sue David for sexual harassment. David's wife, Noreen, hurting deeply and suspecting something fishy, decided to spy on her husband, regardless of her strong moral reservations about breaching trust. Noreen and David's nineteen-year-old son, Richard, flirting with failure at a prestigious engineering institute, convinced himself that cheating on a difficult exam was the only fair thing to do. The twisted string of events is unraveled in David's notebook:

> Shana knew. I didn't say a word but her manner reeked of superficial politeness and cutting sarcasm. We played the doomed lovers' game that night, knowing but not saying, holding reality at bay, making dreams flesh. Tinged with aggression and false reverie, her passion took on a desperate, frantic quality that belied her sweet words. While enmeshed in body, our souls were maneuvering for self-preservation—a treacherous game I knew I would lose in the short run. I was acutely terrified of this person, this brittle doll-woman who still bore the crimson scab of a teardrop carved on her thigh. My scar, she said, for leaving her alone one evening, not loving her enough.
>
> We said our usual good-byes. I walked around the back of her garden apartment to the far edge of the parking lot. I'll never forget the next moment, the moment that my deceptions were given shape and form in a deeply hurt woman, the inevitable moment that my hidden fantasies collided with all that was real and beautiful. When I saw Noreen's car parked next to mine, with a small, dark figure peering out fur-

tively, the cold scalpel of guilt ripped my gut, sever-
ing whatever courage and self-respect that remained.

I panicked. I could not face this lovely woman because I couldn't even grasp who I was at the moment.
Shana's lover was not Noreen's husband. Noreen was
looking in the other direction, so I turned and stum-
bled away, imagining her eyes burning into the nape
of my pitiful neck. I wandered for blocks and finally
caught a cab to a motel, where I sat on the bed in
shock. I prayed that Noreen would not venture over
to Shana's apartment. I called Shana on the pretext of
saying good night again. Nothing unusual, but I could
tell Shana had been crying. Another cut to the heart.

I don't know what most people do when there's
no way out, when they no longer have the energy or
the motivation to climb yet another mountain. For
me, I just started summing it all up in my head—my
childhood, the people I had known, the places I had
been, my job, my marriage. My thinking was grossly
distorted with shame. I felt like an incredible failure,
a marginal human being who could never be anything
more. I truly believed that my family would be better
off without me.

Right now, sitting here, it's hard to imagine I
could be so irrational. I never suspected that matters
of everyday life could push me over the edge. But it's
true. I drank until I could hardly stand and tied a
plastic bag around my head. That's all I remember.
The maid found me the next morning and called an
ambulance. Thank God my clumsy, drunken fingers
botched the job. Apparently I had inadvertently torn
a small hole in the back of the bag.

The thing is, I had an open path but I just didn't
have enough faith to see it—Noreen's love and the
love of my family. I should have trusted her with my
dilemma, even though it meant giving up the fantasy
that I was pursuing, or at least the manner in which

I sought it. Perhaps I wasn't capable or strong enough to do it differently then. Even now, I still don't want to give up the feelings I discovered. But how do I bring them into my "normal" life without going overboard? Even more difficult, how can I feel excited now without re-experiencing the shame? The flashbacks ride on my shoulders, inhibiting every move. After all that's happened, I'm more controlled than ever, even though I don't want to be. With Noreen's help, understanding, and time, perhaps we will find a better balance.

We went through hell during the lawsuit, reliving the intimate details, listening to lies and distortions, fending off the public scrutiny. My—our—humiliation has been unbearable at times. Our bank account is virtually empty but I'm starting a new job with a good friend. The prospects are good.

I cared for Shana very deeply, in spite of what everyone thinks, and wished her no harm. She has gotten the settlement she wanted, but I know it was an empty victory. Her internal battles will go on without me or the next guy who comes along. I would like to believe that we learned a great deal from each other. I doubt if she sees it that way.

Richard was suspended for cheating. There's no excuse but I know that I was part of the dynamic. He lost his way and his priorities got a little screwed up. Sounds familiar. Anyway, as it turns out, we didn't have enough money left to supplement his partial scholarship, and he wouldn't have been able to work enough to foot the steep tuition. He transferred to the state university. To my surprise, he wasn't at all upset about it. Apparently it's where he really wanted to go in the first place but was afraid of disappointing me.

It's hard to speak for Noreen because I can't even comprehend how she has gotten through this. Even during moments of disagreement and conflict, she has never once used the past against me, shamed me in any way, or shown any lingering mistrust. My apologies and amends are expressed in my daily love and respect for her, while her forgiveness is evident in every hug. The resilience amazes me.

I often wonder what would have happened if Noreen hadn't followed me that night. The shock of it triggered my ultimate despair and suicide attempt. But I didn't die and we're back together. Maybe she prevented other horrendous, irreversible acts. As human beings, we may never know the rules that govern the cosmic puzzle.

David is right. We will never know all the rules or the forces that may be operating in any particular situation. Noreen went against her better judgment and followed an intuitive sense. Perhaps she saved the situation, or perhaps she put everyone at unnecessary risk. Maybe it could have been solved by rational discussion, by confronting David more directly. Perhaps Jennifer could have avoided her tragedy by ignoring her boyfriend, Scott, that night or giving up her need for revenge. We'll never know.

Our limited vision in the universal scheme of things is truly daunting. Nevertheless, we must give structure to our consciousness, develop personal and moral awareness, make the best possible, principled decisions that we can, and act on our good intentions. We may never know where each chip will fall, but we will be acting for the good as we understand it, rather than purely selfish needs. The responsibility is enormous yet the personal rewards can be immense. And if you're worried about past misdeeds, it's never too late to rediscover the good person within. The cloak of shame, guilt, fear, anger, and misinformation can be lifted.

ELEVEN

Keys to Rediscovering the Good Person You've Always Wanted to Be

People can and do change: by subtle shifts in values, priorities, and viewpoints or by dramatic transformation. After his ill-fated affair with Shana, David's perspective on life has shifted from a driven, perfectionistic, winners-versus-losers mentality to a broader understanding of himself, other people, and our place in the universal scheme of things. He retains many of his old values but they have been reordered to reflect his new priorities. His attitude is much more open, receptive, and compassionate. Knowledge of his own fallibility has tempered his rather harsh assessment of others. Although he is committed more than ever to his core values, his mind-set is never rigid or dogmatic. He works toward an ever-expanding balance between all that is stable and reliable in his life and his need for spiritual growth.

Shana's sense of fulfillment and vindication was short-lived. The money from her sexual harassment case against David satiated her more immediate needs, but once that was gone, the emptiness returned. Her preoccupation with herself led to a circular, stagnating pattern of thinking and relating that sapped any larger sense of meaning and purpose. At this point, she yearns to escape herself and has found temporary refuge in cocaine and alcohol. She continues to blame David for her difficulties.

After losing her baby and her boyfriend, Scott, fifteen-year-old Jennifer fell into a deep depression and was eventually hospitalized. Once she was free of her infatuations and the group influence, the full force of her transgressions hit home. She had immense difficulty reconciling her acts with her vision of herself. Inside, she was still the innocent little girl. In search of guidance and meaning, she became involved with a local church group. Although still overly susceptible to group influence and the need for a father-figure, Jennifer now espouses more humane values and tries to live her life accordingly. She has no illusions about her capacity to hurt others but is striving to make amends and develop the more positive qualities of her character. She is motivated by a faith in something larger than herself.

What makes people change? If so much seems to be determined by our upbringing and our temperament, what can be changed? Is it ever too late? How does a person go about changing? And why do some people continue to develop morally and spiritually while others languish in stable but stagnant frames of mind? We certainly don't know all the answers to these immensely important questions. But psychologists have gained valuable clues by studying the lives of people who have indeed changed or who have lived their entire lives as a process of transformation. This chapter is based on those findings.

TRANSFORMATIONS

Major life events such as illness, divorce, loss, religious experiences, trauma, marriage, birth, significant accomplishments, and so forth often have the power to change a person's perception of the world and his or her moral priorities. The shift, if any, can be negative and pessimistic or more positive and optimistic. You have undoubtedly seen this in others or experienced it yourself. Something happens that shakes the very core of your self-concept and your assumptions about life.

Like a television that has been kicked, your perceptual filters scramble to tune in and make sense of an array of conflicting new signals. Where have they come from and what lies in between? Suddenly, you may be struck by the humble awareness that your signals are but a small part of a vast, interconnected universe of knowledge, space, and energy. Or, on the contrary, you may be so traumatized that you'll relentlessly hone in on one signal, limiting your perspective to the safe or the familiar. Expecting the worst, you may relate to the world in a more fearful, hostile, or defensive manner. Either way, certain aspects of your personality will remain the same, while other qualities will shift slightly or be applied differently in your life.

Sometimes the shift in perspective comes to us in totally unexpected ways, in spite of ourselves. A turning point is reached as we suddenly find ourselves immersed in a rising sea of larger truths. Oskar Schindler, the subject of the book and film *Schindler's List*, experienced such a turning point. As most of the world knows by now, Schindler, a member of the Nazi party and an opportunist, used Jewish slave labor to run a Polish factory that had been confiscated by the Nazis. Although motivated at the onset primarily by money, self-interest, and power, Schindler's sense of humanity, compassion, and consideration grew as his factory became a merciful refuge from Nazi extermination. Engulfed in something larger than himself, he repeatedly endangered his own life to save others and eventually sacrificed all his worldly possessions. Schindler did not set out to do good, nor was he a particularly virtuous person. Quite the contrary. But, often in spite of himself, his more selfish pursuits diminished as he chose to follow larger principles and truths. This was the turning point that transformed a fallible man into a symbol that will never be forgotten, a testament to the powers of moral choice and responsibility.

Do we need the proverbial kick in the head or the dramatic situation to change our lives? Sometimes we do but it isn't always necessary. For many enlightened souls, the transformation is an ongoing, lifelong process that is not predicated on a dramatic turn of events. These are individuals who aspire to more, who are guided by an expanding sense of meaning and purpose. Their change is gradual and continuous, yet at the same time, they are firmly committed to larger principles. We can learn from their efforts and apply their secrets at any point in our lives. Although our perspectives are likely to solidify more as we age, it's never too late to nudge the tuner.

The Devil's in the Details

How can *you* change? Real change most often comes in small increments. Before looking at the larger visions that may give more meaning and purpose to your endeavors, it's helpful to look again at the small, intimate details of thinking and feeling that make up the daily process of your life. Sustained transformations rely on resilient foundations. You've seen many of these building blocks throughout this book.

Knowing Yourself

Without knowledge of our strengths, weaknesses, and other aspects of our personality, we're doomed to repeat our mistakes. When we avoid, twist, or disguise our shortcomings and hide in a defensive cocoon, we're likely to become unwittingly entangled in a circular, self-defeating process. Psychological defense mechanisms can protect us in times of stress, but they can also lead to habitual, distorted ways of relating to ourselves and others. When they get out of hand, we're apt to shut out shame, guilt, anxiety, and personal liabilities. Disowning part of ourselves can lead to a sense of emptiness, chronic dissatisfaction, and a host of psychological and relationship problems, as well as harm to other people.

As you saw in chapter 6, which addressed the unconscious forces that threaten to lead us astray, psychological defenses such as splitting, denial, projection, dissociation, and acting out all diminish our sense of personal responsibility. Rather than face personal shortcomings or painful truths, we turn a blind eye, disown them, or attribute them to other people. Unfortunately, the information we're trying to avoid can unwittingly seep into other areas of our lives, clouding judgment and undermining our attempts to do the right thing. When this happens, our "basically good" self-concept may become tainted by a nagging sense that something important about ourselves has been lost or compromised. These defensive forces were particularly evident in the lives of Eric, Vanessa's abusive husband, and Shana, David's lover.

Self-knowledge requires an ongoing inventory of your feelings, behaviors, and relationship patterns, as well as the justifications that you employ before and after a course of action. It also requires an interactional style that encourages open feedback between yourself and others whom you trust. You can't change anything unless it's brought to your awareness.

By reflecting on your feelings and motivations, listening to others, and looking at the patterns of your actions and how they affect other people, you will find important clues that belie your defenses. With persistence, you may be rewarded with an enlightening glimpse of the consistent threads running through your personality and character. Some of them will not be particularly helpful or mature. Getting the glimpse is the first step toward change. Along with your Values Profile and your awareness of the elements of good character (see Benchmark 10, page 185), self-knowledge is the basis for a lifelong moral inventory.

Your Values Profile: Striving for a Better Balance

A Values Profile is an informal snapshot of how a person relates to the world in a moral sense. In chapter 4, which addressed how our values may be inconsistent across the social spectrum, you saw how values got out of balance in the lives of Eric and Vanessa, the couple caught in the abusive relationship. There were wide variations in the universal values they subconsciously chose to emphasize, downplay, or disregard in the eight social levels of their lives (self, intimate relationships, family, friends, job, community, country, and society in general). Eric's values in particular were scattered and contradictory. Those he held and aspired to in his friendships (caring, respect, fairness, and loyalty) were totally disregarded in his relationship with Vanessa. Furthermore, his level of social involvement for the larger good was minimal. His moral world was stifling and flat.

Vanessa, on the other hand, did not treat herself as well as she treated other people. She was the eternal rescuer, at great cost to herself. Her commitment to caring was exclusively focused on her troubled husband. It wasn't until she became more receptive to feedback and change that she was able to extend and act upon her good values in other areas of her life. By doing so, she was able to help herself, set goals, expand her boundaries enormously, care for other people, and enrich her experience of the world. Her spiritual life grew because of positive interactions with others whom she respected.

When values such as the Incredible Seven stagnate, distort in small increments, or grossly contradict each other from level to level, a host of psychological and relationship problems can result. No one can apply values consistently across the board, but you should be able to hone in on areas that need work. Periodically, it is helpful to look at each area of your life and determine which values are given priority, if any, and which you may be neglecting. Look at your actions as well as your intentions.

You may find that in spite of your mature stance as an adult, you could be placing a priority on values that were instilled years ago as a child. Vanessa found a long-standing imbalance that had taken shape in childhood and grown imperceptibly as she placed herself in familiar but destructive situations. As is often the case, her life mimicked and reinforced the values that she held, a self-fulfilling cycle.

Overcoming Mind Games: Listening to Feedback, Taking Responsibility

Any attempt to examine, finely tune, or change your life depends upon an ability to truly "see" beyond your self-serving biases and expectations. All of our perceptions and memories have been filtered and biased to varying degrees, however minor, by the time they register in our conscious mind. Our psychological spin doctors thrive on shades of gray and look for compromises that will protect our self-concept or confirm our expectations. As you saw in chapter 5, this can lead to self-deception in the form of distortions, blind spots, believing what we need to believe, and a multitude of excuses to appease ourselves and others. *Our sense of personal responsibility can get lost in the smoke-and-mirrors game.*

To a large extent, this may seem like a Catch-22 situation. How can we see our biases and determine the extent of our responsibility when all we have to rely on is a self-serving lens? The answer, of course, is that we can't always do it alone. *We need other people to challenge our views, question our assumptions, and test our values.*

Whenever we're talking about personal responsibility, we're entering the realm of morality. Morality is interpersonal in nature. In many ways, your moral life is the sum total of all your personal relationships, past and present, good and bad. You've learned from people, even if through their bad examples. Morality develops and grows through personal interaction. It is the give-and-take of relationships— reciprocity, an open mind, and honest communication—that expands perception and spurs moral development. The quality of your relationships and the values of the people you choose to associate with can influence your self-concept, your sense of personal responsibility, and your commitment to moral goals. Few of us are immune from the larger social reality.

This gives rise to another Catch-22. Without honest feedback from people we admire and trust, our thinking is likely to stagnate, our psychological defenses may operate unchecked, and our vision will be limited. But if we do listen to and accept feedback, don't we run the risk of replacing our own distortions with those of other people? Absolutely. In chapter 7, you saw the traps of groupthink: losing ourselves in group values, suspending our critical facilities, and diminishing our personal responsibility.

So what's the answer? Although we may have a dynamic, ever-changing relationship with the world, we must rely on our core ideals, as well as on the qualities of character that sustain an unwavering commitment to those ideals. At the same time, we must continually re-examine our basic attitudes, the beliefs we espouse, and the directions in which we are heading. Our facility for critical thinking should never be placed on extended hold, nor should it become rigid and dogmatic. Life may be a constant interplay between change and stability, but our basic ideas about what is good, fair, honest, and humane reliably chart the course for further exploration. Other people can provide the inspiration and ideas that help us expand and act upon our basic values in new ways. Our core values and our principled goals are the tools for assessing the integrity of their feedback.

Fifteen-year-old Jennifer was overly susceptible to boy-friend Scott's values and criminal group values because she lacked core ideals. She had nothing to strive for other than her own immediate sense of well-being. Her perceptions were easily distorted to rationalize the transgressions she committed. But, as you have seen, distortions can happen even if a person does have core ideals. David's son, Richard, who was caught in the dilemma of whether to cheat on an engineering exam, had many core values but he didn't care enough about honesty and responsibility at that moment to maintain his commitment under pressure. He chose to cheat on the exam and was suspended. His was a lapse of character and conscience rather than a lack of ideals. He truly knew and understood better.

After losing her baby and recovering from a deep depression, Jennifer has since re-evaluated her actions and is working to understand and build upon values such as fairness, responsibility, caring, honesty, respect, loyalty, and liberty. She is allowing herself to feel for and with people again. Although she could point fingers and blame all the negative influences in her life—an erratic, alcoholic mother, abandonment by her stockbroker father, and so forth—she's learning instead to take responsibility for life's choices, regardless of the cards she is dealt. Many things may be grossly unfair and beyond her immediate control, but she is persistent and inspired. As she demonstrates, it's never too late to learn positive values, responsibility, and qualities of good character from other committed individuals. We all need mentors, as well as feedback from our trusted peers and associates. Beware of those who say they don't.

Sharpening Your Moral Sensitivity and Reasoning

Moral Sensitivity.   Empathy lies at the core of moral sensitivity. The capacity to place ourselves in the other person's shoes forms the basis of our motivation to be kind and caring. We know what it feels like to hurt. Although people are born with varying degrees of empathy, it can be enhanced with learning. For most people, problems of moral sensitivity arise not because of a lack of empathy but because they divert, block, or turn it off due to anxiety, anger, fear, hate, or selfishness.

Keeping your moral sensitivity sharp and clear requires a broad-based, generalized empathy that extends to all of humanity, not just to the people you know and care about. This means that you must make a *conscious effort* to understand the feelings, motives, and needs of other people, particularly if they appear to be different. It also means that you must tune in to those subtle pangs of guilt or the slightest reservations you may feel about a certain decision or action. The feelings are a red flag that something may be wrong. If ignored, these vital warnings may be obscured by your justifications and rationalizations. The key is to feel, pay attention, and re-evaluate what you are doing.

Moral Reasoning.   Our moral choices are also guided by our moral reasoning and judgment. Moral reasoning, as you remember, refers to our capacity to understand why some actions may be morally better than others. Although most of our choices and actions are based on moral habits rather than a conscious reasoning process, there are many instances when we are forced to choose between seemingly good alternatives. In those cases, as we sort through the sides of a dilemma, the values at stake, and the rights and needs of others, moral reasoning helps us determine what we ought to do.

You saw the various levels of moral reasoning in Elaine's dilemma over the potentially fraudulent insurance billings and risky treatments at the medical clinic where she works. (See page 159 for specifics.) When Elaine asked members of her therapy group what they thought was the right thing to do, she was surprised by their different perspectives. All of the solutions suggested by the group members were based upon a certain level of "truth" about right and wrong, but some encompassed a broader perspective than others. As the perspective broadened to include larger spheres of influence—from "me" to "us" to ethical principles in general— the priorities and moral imperatives also changed. Elaine was concerned about herself, her fellow employees, and the potential of an insurance investigation, but she was also painfully aware of the larger moral issues. "This whole thing is dishonest. Patients might be at risk, and we're taking advantage of the system and everyone who must pay for it. It's contributing to one of our country's most pressing problems." Some people with a more limited capacity for moral reasoning would never have seen or truly understood this larger perspective.

Our moral reasoning and judgment develop as we learn the reasons behind values, experience the give-and-take of successful relationships, place ourselves in others' shoes, and think through moral conflicts. While some of this happens naturally, it also takes practice and a concerted effort. Laziness is a major impediment to effective moral reasoning. We may not care enough to expend the energy.

While the major building blocks of moral reasoning and judgment are shaped in childhood and early adolescence, it's seldom too late to expand these capabilities. Dramatic changes can occur in the way that you understand the world, your role in it, and your basic assumptions about right and wrong, as well as in the quality of your problem-solving abilities. The key ingredients for enhancing your judgment are: (1) a continuous quest for education and new knowledge; (2) open communication and discussion with others about moral values and ethical dilemmas; and (3) placing yourself in challenging situations where you're exposed to and forced to deal with other perspectives and approaches.

Forgiving and Making Amends

We've heard it a thousand times: holding on to bitterness and anger over past grievances eats away at the spirit and undermines our efforts to seek out new meaning and purpose. Even worse, obsessing over the pain of betrayal often leads to self-righteous, hostile acts of revenge, which only serve to perpetuate the negative cycle.

There is immense wisdom in these age-old observations. It's very easy to lose our sense of goodness if it's obscured by festering wounds that never heal. The problem is, it's very difficult to know when to forgive, either ourselves or others. How do we sort through the various levels of responsibility and decide who or what should be held accountable? Can we forgive without necessarily excusing? Most certainly, we can't always turn the other cheek.

As you saw in chapter 8, which discusses accountability and the problems we may have in seeing and sorting through moral consequences, there are no easy answers here. Forgiveness is an extremely personal, serious act that must be undertaken sincerely and without coercion. However you choose to employ it, you may find that forgiveness will free your spiritual energy, allow you to persist in your goals, and contribute to a positive, optimistic attitude. The actions of other people may hurt, but you will no longer be held hostage by negative ruminations. Even if the past cannot be changed, you have the power to change how it affects you. Learning to forgive, or at the very least, attempting to understand without necessarily excusing, is an important key to rediscovering the good person within.

If you are plagued by guilt over hurting others, the time has come to ask for their forgiveness. If words are insufficient or the injured person is not receptive or available, amends may be in order. Amends are reparations that transform our feelings of remorse into constructive, helpful actions. The negative, self-defeating cycle can be broken by reaching out to help others, either on the personal level or through other broad-based, worthy causes. The good person can be coaxed out again.

ASPIRING FOR MORE: GRAND VISIONS

Many people are indeed very self-reflective, knowledgeable, and morally astute, but nothing really changes in their lives. Their vision tends to stagnate, their goals lapse into the mundane, their thinking takes on a fixed, uninspired quality, and their personal resources are spent pursuing stability and security rather than spiritual growth. They've adapted to or accepted their limitations. They want to be good people, but the range of their action in the world is narrow and only marginally fulfilling.

On the other hand, we've all known or read about very special people who live their lives quite differently. Although aware of their weaknesses, these individuals thrive on certain personal qualities that allow them to engage with and more fully experience the world. This in turn leads them to greater self-awareness, broader horizons, and an ongoing, self-fulfilling process of transformation. They continually place themselves in situations that challenge and expand their capabilities and assumptions. *Their manner of relating to the world and the situations they choose bring about that which they seek.*

What are the powerful personal qualities and visions behind the lifelong transformations? Psychologists Anne Colby
and William Damon (*Some Do Care: Contemporary Lives of
Moral Commitment*, Free Press, 1992) studied the lives of
twenty-three "moral exemplars" from various occupations,
religions, and educational backgrounds. Some of them are
recognized nationally, but most are known primarily in their
local communities. Their activities range from business, jour-
nalism, and education to the human services. Although certainly not saints, martyrs, or zealots, these individuals are
committed to making the world a better place. They were se-
lected for study because they all demonstrated the following
five characteristics:

1. a sustained commitment to moral ideals or principles that include a generalized respect for humanity; or a sustained evidence of moral virtue.
2. a disposition to act in accord with one's moral
   ideals or principles, implying also a consistency
   between one's actions and intentions and between
   the means and ends of one's actions.
3. a willingness to risk one's self-interest for the sake
   of one's moral values.
4. a tendency to be inspiring to others and thereby to
   move them to moral action.
5. a sense of realistic humility about one's own importance relative to the world at large, implying a
   relative lack of concern for one's own ego.

One such individual studied by Colby and Damon was
Suzie Valadez, a sixty-six-year-old women known around El
Paso, Texas, and the Mexican border town of Ciudad Juárez
as "Queen of the Dump." Over the past twenty-eight years,
Suzie has been ministering to the impoverished Mexicans
camping among the rubble and squalor of the huge garbage
dumps surrounding Ciudad Juárez. From her base in El Paso,
she makes the daily trek over the border and spends her

fourteen-hour days handing out food and clothing, organizing volunteers, tending to the two medical clinics she founded, teaching children, and running a charitable mission that she started in 1963. She has been instrumental in raising funds and engaging government agencies, corporations, and large foundations in her efforts.

Although Suzie herself has faced poverty and great hardship, she has worked with unswerving commitment, radiance, and joy. Serving others has been the enriching core of her life. She would have it no other way. In Suzie's view, the love she has given has been returned a thousandfold.

Contrary to what might be expected, Suzie had no training or experience in her endeavors. A tenth-grade dropout with little work experience, she and her four children moved from California to El Paso with a vision to start a mission to help the children of Ciudad Juárez. Struggling as a thirty-eight-year-old single mother in a new town, she had virtually no money and no prospects. With resourcefulness, compassion, a charismatic ability to engage others, and a willingness to take risks, Suzie turned her life around and was able to create the vision that she aspired to.

The idea behind Colby and Damon's study was to find out why Suzie and the other "moral exemplars" are so special, how they got that way, and how they are able to sustain their moral accomplishments and spiritual growth in the face of hardship, opposition, and doubt. Although the findings are complex, there are some striking consistencies from which all of us can learn.

So that we may use these important findings to enhance and enrich our moral lives, they are adapted and presented here as a practical Benchmark. Keep in mind that the generalized statements are based on the lives of individuals who have spent years developing the positive qualities of their characters. Their enduring sense of moral commitment has been forged by many trials and a continuous process of change. It is something we may wish to aspire to. Then again, we may not be prepared for all that is involved.

BENCHMARK NO. 11
TRANSFORMATIONS:
PATHS TO MORAL COMMITMENT AND CHANGE

(Based on the lives of twenty-three "moral exemplars." Adapted from *Some Do Care: Contemporary Lives of Moral Commitment*, by Anne Colby and William Damon.)

1. Moral commitment leads to a focus on causes and concerns that are broader than yourself. To do this, you may have to give up your self-protective stance and place yourself at risk. This is to be expected whenever you attempt to live by your beliefs. There may be personal consequences, but if you are committed, these are of secondary concern. Don't dwell on them.

2. If you are committed, your moral actions are not really a matter of choice or courage. There is great certainty in what you are doing; thus you are not plagued by fear and indecision. Your moral response is natural and without hesitation.

3. By not acting, you risk guilt, self-doubt, or loss of integrity—a situation far worse than the dangers and losses that you might face in carrying out your intentions.

4. Although you are guided by a sense of certainty, it must not become dogmatic. You should persistently seek the truth by opening your mind to new ideas. Continually examine your existing assumptions. Goals and strategies may need to be modified. Your certainty is based on the logical truth but it should always be open to question.

5. Honesty is paramount. You should not compromise the truth to reach certain goals. The means should not compromise the ends. Furthermore,

your commitment to honesty forces you to constantly re-evaluate your other beliefs. Your concern for truth, integrity, and self-improvement will keep you from becoming rigid or dogmatic.

6. If you can suspend your fear and doubt, things have a way of working out. You can create your own future by sticking to your principles. There are dangers in turning away from virtue.

7. Your life is a continuous process of change. You must resist becoming set in your ways. Examine old beliefs, habits, and assumptions and take on new challenges. The stability of your life is provided by a long-term commitment to the principles and causes you believe in.

8. Listen to other people. No matter how strong-minded you may be, you will be powerfully influenced by the perspectives, ideas, and critiques of others. Take guidance from those closest to you, no matter how old or experienced you are.

9. Seek out new challenges and problems rather than avoiding them. These situations provide food for growth. If you don't succeed, it's not terribly important. There are always obstacles and temporary impediments that may defeat you. Concentrate on the positive things you have done and keep trying.

10. If you love and respect other people, they will generally respond in kind, which will make you even more loving. If your efforts are met with hostility and ingratitude, try to avoid becoming bitter or hostile in return. Forgiveness is absolutely necessary to stay on course and persist in your goals.

11. The manner in which you interact with other people is extremely important for moral growth. You will not expand your own capacities unless

you are open, truthful, and self-reflective. Work with other people in an encouraging manner, seek out those who share your fundamental moral goals, listen to alternative perspectives, discuss values, and always strive for new knowledge. You can absorb from others while not losing sight of your own core commitments.

12. Maintain a positive, hopeful attitude but don't ignore reality. Problems are for solving and do not need to be sources of discouragement and despair. Accept them as challenges or turn them to your advantage. Try to make the best of a bad situation. Sometimes you have to consciously decide to be positive in order to circumvent negative or hopeless feelings.

13. Keep a good sense of humor. You're not the world's savior. Although you may be committed, don't take the whole thing or yourself too seriously.

14. A larger sense of meaning and purpose is essential. This may come in the form of religious faith, a personal quest to live an ethical life, a desire for a better world, a need to make social contributions, or any other vision or quest that leads you to focus on the welfare of others. Faith, in a traditional religious sense or not, can hold it all together for you.

While compiling this Benchmark, I was shocked to learn of the brutal murders of two well-intentioned, dedicated young woman at the abortion clinic not far from my home. The individual who perpetrated these atrocities, as well as those who stridently supported his actions, may indeed cite their "moral commitment" as the righteous force behind their woefully misguided efforts.

This is a painful, unfortunate example of how general guidelines and observations, like those cited above, can become twisted and subverted by psychological distortions, blind spots, faulty reasoning, and fanatical group ideals. Pious thoughts and unswerving, rigid commitments to certain ideals do not make a moral exemplar. It is never that simple.

The individuals cited in Colby and Damon's study have all the well-rounded qualities of good character addressed in the previous chapter (see Benchmark 10, page 185). Their goals and the means to pursue them are based on attributes of good character such as openness, honesty, self-awareness, humility, and integrity. These personal qualities developed over time, through years of reflection, interaction, and learning. There are no shortcuts. Zealots and other fanatics often resort to a list of simplistic guidelines or "truths" and make a leap of faith that is totally beyond their personal development and capability. Unfortunately, in their ignorance, they will persist.

MEANING, PURPOSE, AND FAITH

Knowing yourself, sharpening your capacity for critical thought, learning the give-and-take of relationships, and acquiring the practical skills necessary for survival are all worthy goals. But you can achieve many of these objectives and still find yourself floundering in the proverbial sea of uncertainty and dissatisfaction. Where are you going and why are you doing it? Where do you fit in with the world and the universal scheme of things? How do you make sense of life? So what?

By nature, all of us attempt to make sense of what we know and experience. We look for patterns and connections that go beyond the limits of our physical bodies. We're forever organizing and seeking to understand what's going on around us. *It is our understanding of the connections between ourselves and everything else that forms the basis of meaning.* On one level or another, we are always looking for and making meaning.

When the understanding—the meaning—is missing or undeveloped, a natural vacuum forms beneath the surface like a sinkhole, sapping away vitality, hope, and purpose. Your sense of connection will be tenuous or confused, and you will have difficulty defining a place in the world. Relationships may flounder in a dull, stale routine, while your job may never rise above an empty grind. You're a good person, but good for what? Toward what meaning should you invest your life?

Existential angst like this is not just a self-indulgent contrivance of young adults, moral philosophers, and Woody Allen. It's very real for most of us, regardless of our age, intelligence, or education. Sensing the emptiness, we're looking for a unifying belief, a comprehensive vision that encompasses the self and extends to all that is greater. Meaning, when stretched to its largest dimensions, becomes faith.

Faith is what we count on and the truth we follow, in all dimensions of our vision: The sun will rise as it always does, your heart will continue beating while you sleep, others will love and care for you, people can overcome adversity, there can be a better world, there is good in the universe, God is within us, and so forth.

We all have faith in something. The extent and nature of our faith will influence our moral view of existence and our moral behavior, as well as our capacity to live for something greater than ourselves. If we can envision a better world and maintain faith that human beings have the capacity to change it, we may invest our energies in that direction. This in turn can infuse our lives with a vital sense of meaning and purpose. With a broad faith, we are more likely to strive for an ethical life, to follow our most deeply held values. If our faith is limited to the daily mechanics of life, our vision, meaning, and sense of fulfillment will be more circumscribed. We might lose the capacity to dream. We might even give up on our values.

Faith seems to be the strongest when it has religious underpinnings. M. Scott Peck's religious vision is a prime example, illustrating faith in a larger good. In *The Road Less Traveled* (Simon & Schuster, 1978), he explains what he believes to be the meaning of life. In his view, God is our collective unconscious, the extensive, hidden root system, the rhizome that nourishes us all. Our individual consciousness is a tiny plant on the rhizome, with our personal unconscious providing the interface. Inevitably, our conscious self and our unconscious (God) will often be at odds. The ultimate goal is for the individual to become as one with God, to know with God while preserving consciousness. In Peck's own words, "If the bud of consciousness that grows from the rhizome of the unconscious God can become itself God, then God will have assumed a new life form. This is the meaning of our individual existence." We then employ our conscious decisions to become agents of God's grace, creating love, enlightening and helping others to grow to the same plane. Our actions make the presence of God felt in the world.

Faith like this can be a powerful incentive to move beyond selfish concerns and expand our conceptions of moral action and responsibility. Many of the exemplars in Colby and Damon's study shared beliefs similar to those expressed by Peck. By serving others, they found their own inner spirituality, the God within. Thus, they felt an enduring sense of gratitude toward those whom they helped.

As powerful as it may be, religious faith is not necessarily the source of meaning for many enlightened, highly motivated individuals. For them, doing the right thing and living an ethical life form a spiritual quest toward harmony, personal development, and social contribution. Their faith is guided by visions of a better society or by personal interpretations of the transcendent, meaningful forces in the universe.

Regardless of the source of motivation or the vision, we all need dreams to sustain our positive images of ourselves, our world, and our future. The good person within is a well-spring of vitality, hope, and dreams, a powerful resource that can transform the depth and meaning of your life.

While our individual moral development is a vital, primary concern, we can't ignore our larger responsibility as a nation to our own people and the world. Our "national morality" or ethic rests with us but it is expressed through the leaders we choose. Herein lies another dilemma that touches each and every one of us. Knowing what we know about psychological vulnerabilities, lapses in character, blind spots, group foibles, and stunted levels of moral reasoning, what happens when these human weaknesses are coupled with the power to shape and enforce public policy? The values, moral choices, and actions of our leaders have immense repercussions for you, your loved ones, our nation, and the entire world.

A painful example can be found in the dilemma faced by Robert McNamara, the former secretary of defense and "co-architect" of the Vietnam War. Mr. McNamara's dilemma, his attempt at resolution, and the effect on our national conscience encompass some of the greatest moral questions of our time. Tens of thousands of lives rested in his hands while he grappled with the right thing to do. How did this well-intentioned man get lost? Max Frankel, a columnist for the *New York Times Magazine*, captured our collective concern and sense of violation when he asked: "How, without growing cynical, can citizens protect themselves against the stubborn ignorance and misplaced zeal of their leaders?" How indeed?

TWELVE

Leadership, Human Foibles, and the Greater Good: Looking for "Answers"

Vietnam. Watergate. Iran-Contra. Influence-peddling. Kickbacks. Broken promises. Politically motivated deceptions. The seemingly endless violations of public trust, large and small, that we read about or experience daily. It feels as if we're surrounded by a creeping crud, an encroaching fungus that feeds off our cynicism and turns our democratic ideal to mush. The sticky stuff seems to recede after every election, only to return with a vengeance. What's going on with our country and our national esteem?

Throughout this book, we've seen some of the pitfalls and value conflicts that await each of us. Magnify these a quarter billion or more times and we have the collective dilemmas of a democratic nation trying to find its way in an ever-changing moral sea. Our leaders have the daunting task of identifying, articulating, prioritizing, and guiding us through or resolving these dilemmas as they unfold. Furthermore, they must balance their own needs, idiosyncrasies, and personal concerns against the "greater good" of those who have empowered them in the first place. Although the solutions they propose seem pragmatic or technical, moral issues are lurking everywhere. *Can we rely on our leaders to see and make moral decisions? Are we expecting too much of them?* To address these questions, let's look at an important example from our past.

A PAINFUL LESSON

History teaches that our best and brightest routinely succumb to the mundane human foibles that afflict each of us. But unlike most of our slip-ups, the failings of our leaders can have dramatic consequences for millions of lives. Nowhere was this more evident and painful than our country's involvement in Vietnam. To this day, our national conscience twists and turns with haunting memories of the conflict that sparked some of the greatest moral questions of our time. Tens of thousands of Americans and millions of Vietnamese died while our leaders grappled with the best, not necessarily the right, thing to do. Unlike previous wars, right and wrong were obscured in a dank jungle of contradictions, a moral swamp.

Like a traumatized captive held hostage by conflicting needs and values, our collective psyche was irrevocably altered as we battled our internal division, the civil war that played out in the streets of America and the jungles of Vietnam. Was our Vietnam involvement justified to protect our interests against communism, or was it motivated by politics, greed, imperialism, or stupidity? What was the reality of the situation? Could we believe our leaders? Where was our country going? Were we still the good guys? In arguing the pragmatic and moral questions, generations battled, families split, friendships dissolved, and respect for authority vanished. Yet our leaders persisted. Why?

Today, while Vietnam rebuilds itself into an economically viable country, we're still arguing about or denying the degree of our national disgrace, looking for explanations, blaming whatever or whomever we can. The exhausting issue has been raised to consciousness once again by former Secretary of Defense Robert S. McNamara with the publication of his book *In Retrospect: The Tragedy and Lessons of Vietnam* (Times Book/Random House, 1995). We can't refight the Vietnam War here, but McNamara's firsthand account gives us a unique perspective on how well-intentioned leaders go astray.

An intellectually aggressive, no-nonsense hawk and num-ber-cruncher during the Kennedy and Johnson administra-tions, McNamara and a small cohort formulated policies that killed or maimed thousands of young Americans, ripped the soul out of American and Vietnamese families, decimated South Vietnam, and systematically measured "progress" by counting dead bodies. The cohort's justification at the time was to contain the spread of communism in Asia, send a clear message to Russia and China about any further en-croachments, and avoid the devastating nuclear war that could be triggered if these countries weren't held in check. Furthermore, there were U.S. commitments to South Viet-nam dating back to 1954. The commitments had to be hon-ored to preserve diplomatic credibility and power.

To McNamara and his fellow policymakers, the commu-nist uprising in Vietnam was seen as a threat to our national security. Something had to be done. Before 1939, they rea-soned, we had waited too long to confront Hitler. We weren't going to make that mistake again. Furthermore, the limited military intervention proposed for Vietnam had worked in war-torn Korea to prevent a full communist takeover. For McNamara and those who thought they knew all the answers at the time, the actions and sacrifices in Vietnam were justi-fied for the greater good, to protect many more lives down the line. Standard answers, philosophically and technically, were employed for what they perceived as a standard situa-tion—business as usual for a powerful country with God and democracy on its side.

"Mistakes"

To his credit, McNamara now concedes that "we were wrong, terribly wrong" and in his book gives us a blow-by-blow analysis of the technical and logical reasons that the war was doomed to fail. He adds, "I truly believe that we made an error not of values and intentions but of judgment and capabilities." (We'll look at this assertion later.) By now, you may be familiar with his summary of mistakes:

- Misjudging the degree of communist threat to American interests.

- Acting with very little knowledge of Vietnam, the people, their history and culture, and their strong sense of nationalism.

- Viewing the situation exclusively from an American perspective.

- Overestimating what high-tech military forces can accomplish.

- Assuming that the United States had a God-given right to shape every nation in its own image.

- Failure to openly debate the issues with Congress and the American people.

- Believing that immediate, tidy answers can be found for all problems.

McNamara began to have serious doubts back in 1965 about the chances of winning the war and questioned U.S. policy in a series of unsuccessful internal memos to President Lyndon B. Johnson. Johnson, behaving as an autocratic leader and intent on protecting his domestic agenda, continued to believe that forceful intervention would more quickly bring the North Vietnamese to the table. Ho Chi Minh, the communist leader, could be bombed into submission without disrupting Johnson's legacy, the Great Society. Although a reluctant player, McNamara nevertheless felt an obligation to obey his president. In pursuit of misguided objectives the Johnson administration, like the Nixon administration which followed, turned a deaf ear to dissent and embarked on a policy of public deception and misrepresentation. The American public at large had little inclination to doubt the distorted information they were being fed.

Disillusioned and caught in a conflict of loyalty with Johnson, McNamara left his position (or was gently fired) in 1968. Although his dissenting views were leaked to the press with his knowledge and approval, and published as part of the Pentagon Papers in 1971, McNamara remained silent in the public arena. The war machine churned on for seven brutal years after he left the Pentagon.

With the publication of his book, McNamara has been severely criticized for not speaking up sooner with more conviction. In response, he cites the limitations and expectations of his former role as an unelected cabinet officer. "Every cabinet officer must do as the president says or get the hell out. And if he gets out, he cannot attack the president from outside the cabinet, essentially using the power given to him by the president." He further believes that his voice wouldn't have made any positive difference after he left office, and in fact could have undermined the efforts of those attempting to negotiate an end to the war.

Knee Deep in the Big Muddy

Knowing what we know about the human foibles that influence or undermine our moral vision, what can we make of all this? First and foremost, we must not unduly blame or scapegoat our well-meaning former secretary of defense. His shortcomings were compounded by a national attitude that prevailed at the time and reflected some serious flaws in government ethics and leadership. The flaws continued to mutate into the spectacles of Watergate and Iran-Contra. Furthermore, in spite of thousands of active demonstrations against the war, Americans as a whole allowed their leaders to continue. In the eyes of the world, we have a collective responsibility in the Big Muddy.

Coming Clean

Before continuing, what is my personal bias? What part did I play in the miserable mess? While three million Vietnamese were being blown to bits by sustained U.S. bombing and young Americans were returning home in body bags or or stretchers, I was working full time in psychiatric hospitals and studying at Arizona State University. Vietnam was the central, most divisive issue on campus as we clung to our student deferments. We marched, held candlelight vigils, debated the issues endlessly, occupied the Reserve Officers' Training Corps (ROTC) building, and shamelessly provoked the National Guard. The university's Board of Regents were "pigs." "We" had a certain mind-set that danced on the edge of self-righteous groupthink. The feelings were powerful, the cause greater than ourselves.

I listened skeptically as my peers talked about a new moral order of peace, love, and cooperation, but went along for the fantasy. I withdrew when too many fell into an "us-them" mentality, blindly attacking local shopkeepers and carrying out other destructive acts against the "Establishment." As my hair reached to my shoulders, I was kicked out of the mandatory ROTC courses after meticulously filling in exam answer sheet grids to form Christmas tree patterns. The colonel shook his head in disgust: In his opinion, I was making a serious mistake that would jeopardize my career and come back to haunt me. I would never be a shake 'n' bake second lieutenant in Vietnam. Unlike many, at least I had some semblance of choice.

I dropped my student deferment for a year, sweating it out, counting on my borderline lottery number. My roommate paid a draft doctor $100, smoked nonstop prior to his induction physical, and bled profusely when needles were stuck: 4F or some other magic number. My brother, a brilliant philosopher, went to Canada after the Secret Service filmed his graduation from Bucknell. He disappeared out of my life for twenty years. Other people also vanished from the United States or were killed in Vietnam.

Our lives were torn apart but joined by a common plaint. For many of us, the essence of our young adulthood was developed and defined by an adversarial relationship with our country, authority in general, and our confused parents. Like children in a grossly dysfunctional family, our personal issues were deflected and largely ignored as we struggled with the massive denial and avoidance of those in power. The immaturity that prevailed was destructive and often deadly, even on the homefront. And now we're told it was a big mistake, an error in judgment and capability. Is this new? The mistakes cited by McNamara were pointed out years ago by thousands of Americans and leaders the world over. Their words and were dismissed as ill-informed, naive, moralistic, or cowardly.

No, I never served in Vietnam. But as a therapist working with returning veterans, I listened to and felt elements of their profound pain, frustration, rage, and moral guilt; I was drawn into the absurdity of their daily hell and boredom, the highs and horrors of discovering one's own lethal capabilities, the overwhelming sense of betrayal when the truth and folly of the war spat in their faces. I agonized that my anti-war activities might have caused them even more grief. And a couple of years ago, a lifelong friend who avoided the draft and protested like the rest of us in his long ponytail and tie-dyed shirt informed me that it was a big mistake. He fervently wished that he had gone to Vietnam. "I was ignorant, caught up by the naive hysteria of our generation. I missed something important in the process." *Say what?*

For those of you who are hell-bent on categorizing my political proclivities, I'll confound the issue by telling you that, as a teenager in Arizona, I actively campaigned for Barry Goldwater in his Senate race. To this day, I have immense respect for his character and independence of mind, if not for his more historical views. Go figure. Such is the limitation of thinking in broad categories. The issues we're addressing here go beyond political orientations.

I do not know Robert McNamara personally but I respect his efforts, limited as they may be, to share what he has learned. I do not believe that atonement and a need for forgiveness were his motives for writing the book; his thinking may be far too pragmatic and technical for him to really hear or feel the meaning behind such soft words. Although his prickly manner and incisive words are possibly belied by his welcome tears, it is extremely difficult to know what rests within his well-guarded conscience and heart. Here is a man who appears to be embarrassed by his own emotions.

Ron Kovic, the paraplegic vet who wrote *Born on the Fourth of July*, posed a challenge to us all when he said recently, "Over the long run, McNamara's book and his comments will promote healing. As Americans, we must all embrace McNamara. We must all welcome him home." Something to think about as we wade through the whys of Vietnam and the human foibles of our leaders.

The Dollar Auction Game

As we continue our brief excursion through the big muddy, let's look at a psychological trap that has little to do with morality, but plays a role in certain errors of judgment. Highly intelligent, capable leaders like Robert McNamara and Lyndon Johnson have been snared. Psychologist Martin Shubik devised a clever game to illustrate the power of the trap. It goes as follows. A dollar bill is being auctioned off to the highest bidder. You, a hopeful bidder, are given four simple rules:

1. You may not communicate with any of the other bidders while the auction is in progress.
2. All bids must be made in increments of five cents—5 cents, 10 cents, 15 cents, 20 cents, etc.
3. So that you don't get carried away (ha, ha), the maximum bid is $50.
4. Here's the kicker. Although the dollar goes to the highest bidder, the second highest bidder *also* has to pay what he or she bids, getting nothing in return. This money goes to the auctioneer to pay for his services and reduce his potential loss.

The game begins. The bidding starts with a nickel and builds to 35 cents. You counter with 40 cents. Another person bids 45 cents. Someone else says 50 cents. So far, so good. The bidding slows. Hopeful, you go for 55 cents. But watch out. At this point, you could get a dollar for 55 cents but the collective investment in the game is $1.05, the sum of what you and the second highest bidder must shell out. The auctioneer would make a nickel profit. Thus, as each bidder pursues individual interests, the cost of the dollar goes up.

But who cares about the collective cost? Your share is less than $1.00 and you could still come out ahead. The bidding proceeds and works its way up to 90 cents, just you and some doofus wearing a torn-up old T-shirt. You say 95 cents, he shouts "a dollar." *What? Is he really crazy enough to bid a dollar for a dollar?* But now you have a problem. If you fold up and go home, you'll lose 95 cents (the second highest bid goes to the auctioneer). *This idiot is forcing me to bid $1.05! But at least I'd lose only a nickel instead of 95 cents.* You bid $1.05, the doofus shouts "$1.10." *Man, I don't believe this guy. He must be into this macho thing or something, trying to prove a point. Some people!* You shout "$1.15." The game goes on and your potential losses escalate. *He looks as if he doesn't have money to throw away. He's got to give up at some point.*

The problem is, the doofus is thinking the same thing as you and can't figure out why you don't just cut your losses and walk. He's angry as hell and blames you for the situation. He can't afford to pull out now and is more committed than ever to his course of action, even though he is digging a deeper and deeper hole.

If the insanity continues to the maximum bid of $50, someone will walk away with the dollar bill for $50—a $49 loss—while the other person will shell out $49.95 to the auctioneer. Someone other than you and the doofus is making out like a bandit.

When the dollar auction game is played out in real life with experimental subjects, the bidding typically reaches a few dollars. Each final bidder becomes exasperated with and blames the other, even though their predicaments are identical. Since communication is not allowed, compromises are not discussed. Saving face also becomes important, depending upon the personalities of the bidders.

The entrapments found in this simple game certainly are not identical with those that perpetuated the Vietnam War, but there are striking similarities. It's easy to see how non-communicative, determined leaders might escalate their commitment to a failing course of action even as their losses mount. These dynamics may very well have applied to President Lyndon Johnson as he took on the war as his own, stifled debate within Congress (most of whose members willingly conceded), bullied those who disagreed, and sought technical solutions to clobber Ho Chi Minh into quick submission. A decisive victory seemed possible. The leader of North Vietnam had different ideas.

By 1967, Robert McNamara saw the folly and privately challenged Johnson and his colleagues on pragmatic rather than on moral grounds. His views were rejected. The agenda that he helped formulate had taken on a life of its own. As Americans watched the undeniable bloodshed on TV for the first time, Johnson lost control of public opinion, the war, and his presidency.

Enter Richard Nixon, who suppressed domestic opposition, engaged the FBI and CIA to investigate dissenters, authorized secret bombings in neutral Cambodia, used whatever means he could to justify his often paranoid ends, and repeatedly lied to the public. All for, in his words, "peace with honor." His failings went far beyond "errors in judgment" and set the pervasive tone for an executive branch gone haywire.

Even Tougher Issues

Where do we draw the line when we talk about "errors in judgment"? For example, since Adolf Eichmann actually believed that Jews were everything evil his fellow Nazis painted them to be, were his heinous war crimes errors of judgment? Or did they reflect a deeper perversion of values and character? In this extreme example, the answer is quite clear for most people. But certainly, this is not always the case.

Consider Robert McNamara's recent assertion about Vietnam. I don't mean to single him out, but he has courageously put himself on the line so that we may learn from his trials. He states, *"I truly believe that we made an error not of values and intentions but of judgment and capabilities."* This is a hard nut to crack. Does it ring true?

As you saw in the dollar auction game, errors in judgment can and do happen in contexts relatively free of values and moral considerations. But if you're bidding for the dollar with human lives, the situation takes on dramatic new implications. With every new bid, you are sending thousands of people to their graves, cutting a wide swath in the web of humanity. Every decision has immense moral consequences. Every decision reflects the values that you choose to emphasize or downplay regarding life and death, definitions of the greater good, personal and collective responsibility, and so forth.

Given the stakes involved, a person choosing different values may have diligently questioned his or her assumptions and invited debate. A person with different values and greater self-knowledge may not have gotten caught up in the threat of losing face. A person acting on different values may have fervently challenged or broken the rules of the game, in spite of the personal consequences. A person choosing different values may never have entered the auction in the first place, even if "winning" seemed likely.

The policies followed by McNamara and his colleagues reflected the values that were very much a part of the American ethic at the time. Communism was to be defeated or contained at all costs, military solutions to problems were more readily employed, Congress and the public deferred more to the president in matters of foreign policy, American perspectives were always best, and the United States had a God-given right to shape developing nations, including Vietnam.

Many of the "errors in judgment" cited by McNamara (see page 221) did, in fact, stem from rather shaky values. Vietnam was not a technical problem that could be solved with military hardware and rules of foreign negotiation. It was a war of values, assumptions, and attitudes. Difficult moral assessments were required that transcended the "expertise" and knowledge of Lyndon Johnson, Robert McNamara, or any group of politicians. By keeping the decision-making process secret, they excluded the American people and circumvented the moral debate. They shielded us from responsibility, when in fact only we could have made the tough decisions about our nation's role in the world. Only we could have determined whether we wanted to sacrifice our children for certain beliefs. But by the time we had a chance to examine our values and objectives, we were knee deep in the Big Muddy, buying our way out with more human lives.

To this day, McNamara continues to sidestep the difficult moral issues. He fails to address our government's duplicity, the betrayal of our young soldiers, the right and wrong of dominating ("rescuing") a country to fulfill our own vision, the merciless killing and destruction that went on in the name of an ill-defined objective, the courtship that was allowed to escalate into a brutal rape when we didn't get our way. It is especially disappointing that McNamara has not been able or willing to adequately address his own moral failure. Perhaps there are many things as yet unresolved in his own mind.

While I have little doubt that Robert McNamara sweated blood and tears over his decisions, his assessment of the situation is curiously blunted in feeling and personal insight. In fact, he never really addresses the *personal* tragedies of Vietnam, his own included. We don't quite know his private feelings and are left to wonder if he shut them out when making decisions in his *role* as secretary of defense.

So many questions remain unanswered. Were his moral sensitivities diminished by his role? Did his loyalty to the president obscure his broader vision? Was he intimidated by Johnson or in need of his approval? As a can-do manager, did he get carried away with objectives and statistics? Why weren't basic assumptions questioned before putting so much on the line? And why couldn't he *really* hear other voices, including those emanating from his own family? Was it a blip in personality or character? We'll probably never know. His observations today, like his solutions yesterday, continue to be predominantly factual and technical. Perhaps this is the very best he can do, at least in public. Indeed, we may be asking too much of him.

But regardless of Robert McNamara's inability to answer our questions, he cannot escape our moral gaze. There are moral absolutes that go beyond his words and his reasons. He tells us that he did not forcefully speak up after leaving the Pentagon—after seeing the flaws in policy that were sending thousands to their graves—because to do so would have violated the rules. Cabinet officers, in or out of office, do not publicly attack their president. He states, "I recognize this is not a widely accepted view, but I believe it's the correct view—grounded in the Constitution and shared by such former cabinet officers as Dean Acheson." He also tells us that his voice wouldn't have made a difference, and furthermore, it might have undermined diplomatic efforts to end the war.

Something is wrong here. In chapter 5, we saw how pervasive our blind spots can be, particularly when they are fueled by unrecognized emotions such as fear, anxiety, or anger. We saw the gamut of excuses and rationalizations: minimizing the consequences and implications of an act; justifying; saying that everyone does it; claiming mitigating circumstances, and so on. When you read Mr. McNamara's statements, what is your initial gut reaction? Is there a moral failure here clouded by rationalizations?

To put this dilemma into perspective, imagine that you

were chosen by a prestigious engineering firm to design a suspension bridge across the Delaware River. Halfway through
the construction project and millions of dollars later, you
discover a design flaw that could lead to the failure of the
steelwork. You're not absolutely certain about it, but the
probabilities of collapse are very high. Hundreds of travelers
could die, the engineering firm would be sued, and you
could be held responsible. You take your discovery to your
boss, and he disagrees with your assessment. Besides, it's too
late to change the design without tearing down everything
that's already been done. A financial and political disaster.

Night after night, like Robert McNamara, you sweat. You
question your assessments and your convictions. Finally,
you leave the project in mid-course and move on to something else, knowing that your friends and loved ones will be
traveling over that bridge nearly every day.

What would *you* do?

Is there anyone reading this who wouldn't speak out, in
fact, shout the truth from the hills? Would you be satisfied
with a few newspaper articles written by nonengineers that
question the safety of the bridge? And if you didn't speak
out, is there anything at all that could possibly defend your
moral failure?

Most certainly, we all fail at times. I, like you, know that
very well. It's all too easy to judge others when we're not in
their shoes. But sometimes the truth simply cannot be ignored. It's quite sad that Mr. McNamara still does not see or
acknowledge the extent of his personal failure. He appears to
be a well-intentioned, good man who can't grasp the magni-
tude of his omissions. His forcefully persistent voice could
have changed the course of history. Perhaps the degree of
courage that enables him to write today will indeed have an
impact on tomorrow. We can continue to learn from what he
says, as well as from what he does not say.

To analyze Mr. McNamara's psyche any further without
sufficient information would do him a great disservice. It's
safe and easy to size up others when our own neck has never

felt the bite of such an immense noose. In spite of his human foibles and fallibilities, he has never stopped looking for answers or questioning himself. Rich Rusk, son of former Secretary of State Dean Rusk, aptly reminds us of this fact in the *Washington Post*:

> Of that small circle who made Vietnam policy in the '60s [including Dean Rusk], only one was able to stare into the abyss, challenge his own assumptions and confront that horrible question:
> "What if I am wrong?"
> That man was Robert McNamara.

These observations aside, we may never agree, as a nation or as individuals, how much to hold McNamara accountable or whether forgiveness is warrented. Either way, we need to look at the larger picture. Our future depends upon it.

OUR LEADERS, OURSELVES: WHAT CAN WE EXPECT?

As you know only too well, the Vietnam conflict is only one example of leadership run amok. The human dynamics that fueled the war have been with us for eons and will continue in the future. But part of the difficulty lies with us, the voters, and our quest for "answers." Like many of the politicians we elect, we don't seem to realize that the problems we face cannot always be answered with clear-cut, practical solutions. As in the Vietnam dilemma, our problems and questions often reflect deeper needs and conflicting values. Quick-fix technical solutions alone simply will not work in the long run.

Looking Beyond the Big Fix

If your throbbing tooth has a cavity, you'll authorize a dentist to diagnose and treat the problem. In most cases, he or she will know exactly what to do. The problem has been faced many times before, and standard procedures may be used. The rules and expectations are clear. The problem is concrete, the answer is technical, and the burden of responsibility is on the dentist. If something goes wrong, you know who to blame. This is how many of us relate to our elected officials. We challenge them with issues that appear to be technical, like the environment or the "war" on drugs, expect them to have ready answers, and chastise them if they don't. The media is particularly brutal in this regard.

If you're mildly depressed and seek out a therapist, the situation becomes slightly more complicated. The therapist is the "authority," yet the lines of responsibility are not so clear. Depending upon your expectations and the orientation of the therapist, he could tell you what's wrong, give you Prozac, make suggestions about your problems, and send you on your way. The therapist offers answers. This may work for some cases but not for others. Perhaps you have some personal dilemmas involving guilt, shame, or the right thing to do. A well-trained therapist will know that he cannot make those determinations for you. He can only help you to discover and sort through the underlying conflicts and values. But if *you* don't understand the limitations of his role, you'll probably fire him—that is, you will walk away.

Consider a more complicated situation. If your community has a wave of burglaries, you and your neighbors may decide to take some responsibility for preventing them and form a neighborhood crime watch. Even though a police officer may help you form the group, chances are you'll choose one strong-minded individual to act as leader. She will be given special authority while the rest of you assume various secondary roles. You may expect the leader to articulate the problem, define tasks, and provide direction. This reduces stress and builds a sense of cohesion. If something goes wrong, you know where to go. The leader, in turn, maintains authority only as long as she continues to handle problems effectively. Just like your dentist, she must come up with certain "answers."

Your neighborhood watch leader may do very well when asked about assignments, the specifics of home security, and coordination with the police force. These questions are basically technical. But what happens if your ever-expanding group decides to get at the heart of the crime in your community? You'll want to know all possible "causes." Perhaps your leader will consult with various experts and other citizen groups. They're likely to have many different opinions about the nature of the problem and possible solutions. Some may blame an influx of illegal immigrants. Others may point to drug abuse. Still others may blame cultural and economic conditions. The demise of family values may also be cited. Solutions will be proposed, with each one reflecting certain values, beliefs, and attitudes. Some of the solutions will be expensive or may require uncomfortable changes for the community. Others will simply scapegoat and blame.

At this point, your leader may feel buffeted about and lost. What is she to do? Your group is expecting some sort of direction. She fears that if she puts all the issues on the table, the group will become overwhelmed, frustrated, and splintered. Valuable time could be squandered in divisiveness. Furthermore, as the heat grows, the group members could blame her for ineffective leadership, for not telling them what is best. They might even call for her resignation.

To safeguard her authority and avoid abstractions that could lead to arguments, she decides to present her own "position paper" rather than the jumble of diverging views. Even though she's far from certain about the possible solutions, she argues for a dramatic increase in the police force. She wants to convey a sense of decisiveness. And if she backs off from the paper as her thinking changes or evolves, she'll be seen as "waffling." This is a double bind that plagues many leaders.

While an authoritative leadership approach like this may work for the dentist, it is not helpful for your neighborhood group. "Crime," unlike a cavity, is not a specific problem with a specific solution. Crime always has been and always will be a part of human society. Like the personality of an obnoxious relative, no one really knows what to do about it. Few leaders have the courage to admit this simple fact. In your neighborhood group, small, practical steps can indeed be taken, but those steps must be determined over time, with soul-searching and debate about all the competing values and costs. Your leader, like the therapist, cannot provide all the answers here. She can help only to raise and process the difficult questions, adding whatever technical expertise she has along the way. Your community has some tough decisions to make. A series of open meetings could be the first step.

Our Responsibility

Unfortunately, most of us are too impatient and uninvolved to allow our leaders to function as explorers and facilitators when our country is faced with value-laden questions. We'll accuse them of skirting the issues. We'll vote for someone else who is more outspoken and definitite. We'll complain about the government encroaching upon our lives but avoid our own responsibility. We'll claim that the issues are far too complex, and with our limited access to the technical ins and outs, we're in no position to debate.

But as we have seen with Vietnam, all the technical knowledge in the world, all the nitty-gritty knowledge of foreign diplomacy, tactics, and political maneuvers, served only to obscure the larger issues and tough choices. The experts we empowered, in spite of their extensive experience, could make ethical decisions no better than you or me.

The powers and structures of democracy provide the arena in which to examine our values and our national priorities. Most certainly, we vote for those who reflect our values and beliefs. But as we have seen throughout this book, the values that you or our leaders choose to emphasize may change dramatically from situation to situation. The values of democratic leadership and human rights that Lyndon

Johnson emphasized in his domestic accomplishments were grossly neglected in his foreign policy. We cannot trust our leaders to make the big decisions alone—not because they don't necessarily warrant trust, but because they are human.

Leadership requires the ability to step back from a problem, look at the patterns, and determine whether the problem involves larger values and attitudes that must be examined, debated, and possibly changed. Nuts-and-bolts answers to problems of value and belief are no answers at all. Strong citizenship requires realistic expectations of our leaders, sharing of responsibility, a continuous examination of our values and priorities, and an active, informed voice. It also requires all the components of moral knowing, moral feeling, and moral action that we have explored throughout this book. Our political leaders cannot do this for us. As citizens of a democratic nation, we must look *within* and *beyond* ourselves when the moral seas rise.

BIBLIOGRAPHY

Alter, Jonathan. "I Sweated Blood at Night About It." (An interview with Robert McNamara). *Newsweek*, April 17, 1995:52–53.

Baumeister, Roy. "Lying to Yourself: The Enigma of Self-Deception." In *Lying and Deception in Everyday Life*, edited by Michael Lewis and Carolyn Saarni. New York: Guilford Press, 1993.

————. "The Optimal Margin of Illusion." *Journal of Social and Clinical Psychology*. 1989, 8:171–89.

Baumeister, Roy, and S. R. Wotman. *Breaking Hearts: The Two Sides of Unrequited Love*. New York: Guilford Press, 1992.

Baumrind, D. "Current Patterns of Parental Authority." *Developmental Psychology Monographs*. 1971, vol. 4.

Bellah, R., R. Madsen, W. Sullivan, et al. *The Good Society*. New York: Knopf, 1991.

Bellah, R., R. Madsen, A. Swidler, et al. *Habits of the Heart: Individualism and Commitment in American Life*. New York: Harper & Row, 1985.

Bergin, A. "Values and Religious Issues in Psychotherapy and Mental Health." *American Psychologist*. 1991, 46(4): 394–403.

Berkowitz, B. *Local Heroes: The Rebirth of Heroism in America*. Lexington, Mass.: Lexington Books, 1987.

Blasi, A. "Moral Cognition and Moral Action: A Theoretical Perspective." *Developmental Review*. 1983, 3:178–210.

Bok, Sissela. *Lying: Moral Choice in Public and Private Life*. New York: Pantheon Books, 1978.

Caspi, A., and D. Bem. "Personality Continuity and Change Across the Life Course." In *Handbook of Personality: Theory and Research*, edited by L. Pervin. New York: Guilford Press, 1990.

Chess, S., and A. Thomas. *Temperament and Development*. New York: Brunner Mazel, 1977.

Church, George, Bruce Nelan, Tobias Wolff, et al. "Re-Examining a Wound That Won't Heal." *Time*, April 24, 1995: 22–48.

Clinard, M. *Corporate Ethics and Crime: The Role of Middle Management*. Beverly Hills, Cal.: Sage, 1983.

Colby, Anne, and William Damon. *Some Do Care: Contemporary Lives of Moral Commitment*. New York: Free Press, 1992.

Colby, Anne, and Lawrence Kohlberg. *The Measurement of Moral Judgment*. New York: Cambridge University Press, 1987.

Damon, William. *The Moral Child*. New York: Free Press, 1988.

Damon, William, and Anne Colby. "Social Influence and Moral Change." In *Moral Development Through Social Interaction*, edited by W. Kurtines and M. Gewirtz. New York: Wiley, 1987.

Dixon, N. *Preconscious Processing*. New York: Wiley, 1981.

Doob, Leonard. *Panorama of Evil: Insights for the Behavioral Sciences*. Westport, Conn.: Greenwood, 1978.

Draper, Theodore. "The Abuse of McNamara." *New York Review*. May 25, 1995.

Eisenbergh, N. *The Roots of Prosocial Behavior in Children*. New York: Cambridge University Press, 1989.

Epstein, S. "The Self-Concept: A Review and the Proposal of an Integrated Theory of Personality." In *Personality: Basic Issues and Current Research*, edited by Ervin Staub. Englewood Cliffs, N.J.: Prentice-Hall, 1980.

Forward, Susan. *Toxic Parents*. New York: Bantam, 1989.

Fowler, J. *Stages of Faith: The Psychology of Human Development and the Quest for Meaning*. San Francisco: Harper & Row, 1981.

Frankel, Max. "McNamara's Retreat." *New York Times Book Review*, April 16, 1995.

Freud, Sigmund. "Repression." In *The Standard Edition of the Complete Works of Sigmund Freud*, vol. 15, edited by J. Strachey. London: Hogarth Press, 1957.

——— . *The Ego and the Id*. London: Hogarth Press, 1927.

Gavrin, E. "Moral Choice." In *Moral Development Through Social Interaction*, edited by W. Kurtines and M. Gewirtz. New York: Wiley, 1987.

Gilligan, C. *In a Different Voice*. Cambridge, Mass.: Harvard University Press, 1982.

Goffman, Erving. *Frame Analysis*. Cambridge, Mass.: Harvard University Press, 1974.

——— . *The Presentation of Self in Everyday Life*. New York: Doubleday, 1959.

Goleman, Daniel. *Vital Lies, Simple Truths: The Psychology of Self-Deception*. New York: Simon & Schuster, 1985.

Greenwald, A. "Self-Knowledge and Self-Deception." In *Self-Deception: An Adaptive Mechanism?* edited by J. Lockard and D. Paulhus. Englewood Cliffs, N.J.: Prentice-Hall, 1988.

Hallie, Philip. "Cruelty: The Empirical Evil." In *Facing Evil: Light at the Core of Darkness*, edited by Paul Woodruff and Harry Wilmer. La Salle, Ill.: Open Court Publishing Company, 1988.

Harper, J., and M. Hoopes. *Uncovering Shame*. New York: Norton, 1990.

Heifetz, Ronald A. *Leadership Without Easy Answers*. Cambridge, Mass.: Harvard University Press, 1994.

Hodgson, Kent. *A Rock and a Hard Place: How to Make Ethical Business Decisions When the Choices Are Tough*. New York: AMACOM, 1992.

Hoffman, M. L. "Empathy, Guilt, and Social Cognition." In *The Relationship Between Social and Cognitive Development*, edited by W. F. Overton. Hillsdale, NJ: Lawrence Erlbaum, 1983.

———. "Empathy, Role-Taking, Guilt, and Development of Altruistic Motives." In *Moral Development and Behavior: Theory, Research, and Social Issues*, edited by Thomas Lickona. New York: Holt, Rinehart & Winston, 1976.

———. "Empathy, Social Cognition, and Moral Education." In *Approaches to Moral Development*, edited by A. Garrod. New York: Teachers College Press, 1993.

Hunt, Morton. *The Compassionate Beast: What Science Is Discovering About the Humane Side of Humankind*. New York: William Morrow, 1990.

Janis, Irving. *Victims of Groupthink*. Boston: Houghton Mifflin, 1983.

Janoff-Bulman, R. "The Aftermath of Victimization: Rebuilding Shattered Assumptions." In *Trauma and Its Wake*, edited by C. Figley. New York: Brunner Mazel, 1985.

Kagan, Jerome. *The Nature of the Child*. New York: Basic Books, 1984.

Kaufman, G. *Shame: The Power of Caring*. Cambridge, Mass.: Schenkman, 1985.

Kelman, Herbert, and V. Lee. Hamilton. *Crimes of Obedience: Toward a Social Psychology of Authority and Responsibility*. New Haven, Conn.: Yale University Press, 1989.

Kitwood, T. *Concern for Others*. London: Routledge, 1990.

Kohlberg, Lawrence. *Essays on Moral Development: The Psychology of Moral Development*, vol. 2. San Francisco: Harper & Row, 1984.

———. "Moral Stages and Moralization: The Cognitive Developmental Approach." In *Moral Development and Behavior*, edited by Thomas Lickona. New York: Holt, Rinehart and Winston, 1976.

———— . *The Philosophy of Moral Development: Moral Stages and the Idea of Justice*. New York: Harper & Row, 1981.

Kurtines, W., and J. Gerwirtz. *Morality, Moral Behavior, and Moral Development*. New York: Wiley, 1984.

Lamb, S. "The Beginnings of Morality." In *Approaches to Moral Development*, edited by A. Garrod. New York: Teachers College Press, 1993.

Langdale, S. "Moral Development, Gender Identity, and Peer Relationships in Early and Middle Childhood." In *Approaches to Moral Development*, edited by A. Garrod. New York: Teachers College Press, 1993.

Lerner, M. *The Belief in a Just World: A Fundamental Delusion*. New York: Plenum, 1980.

Lickona, Thomas. *Educating for Character: How Our Schools Can Teach Respect and Responsibility*. New York: Bantam Books, 1991.

———— . *Raising Good Children*. New York: Bantam Books, 1983.

Luks, A. *The Healing Power of Doing Good*. New York: Ballantine, 1992.

Lyons, N. "Two Perspectives: On Self, Relationships, and Morality." *Harvard Educational Review*. 1983, 53:125–45.

McKay, Matthew, P. Rogers, and J. McKay. *When Anger Hurts: Quieting the Storm Within*. Oakland, Cal.: New Harbinger, 1989.

McNamara, Robert S. *In Retrospect: The Tragedy and Lessons of Vietnam*. New York: Times Books/Random House, 1995.

Millon, Theodore. *Disorders of Personality*. New York: Wiley, 1982.

Morrison, A. "Shame, Ideal Self, and Narcissism." In *Essential Papers on Narcissism*, edited by A. Morrison. New York: International Universities Press, 1989.

Nicholas, Mary W. *The Mystery of Goodness and the Positive Moral Consequences of Psychotherapy*. New York: Norton, 1994.

Parks, Sharon. *The Critical Years: Young Adults and the Search for Meaning, Faith, and Commitment*. San Francisco: Harper & Row, 1986.

Peck, M. Scott. *People of the Lie: The Hope for Healing Human Evil*. New York: Simon & Schuster 1983.

———— . *The Road Less Traveled: A New Psychology of Love, Traditional Values and Spiritual Growth*. New York: Simon & Schuster, 1978.

Peck, R., and R. Havighurst. *The Psychology of Character Development.* New York: Wiley, 1960.

Piaget, J. *The Moral Judgment of the Child.* New York: Free Press, 1965.

Reimer, Joseph, D. Paolitto, and R. Hersh. *Promoting Moral Growth: From Piaget to Kohlberg.* 2nd ed. New York: Longman, 1983.

Rest, James. *Moral Development: Advances in Research and Theory.* New York: Praeger, 1986.

————. "Morality." In *Manual of Child Psychology*, edited by P. Mussen. New York: Wiley, 1983.

Rokeach, M. *Beliefs, Attitudes, and Values.* San Francisco: Jossey-Bass, 1968.

————. *The Nature of Human Values.* New York: Free Press, 1973.

Rusk, Rich. "Did He Help with the Healing?" *Washington Post*, April 26, 1995.

Ryan, Kevin, and George McClean. *Character Development in Schools and Beyond.* New York: Praeger, 1987.

Saarni, Carolyn, and Michael Lewis. "Deceit and Illusion in Human Affairs." In *Lying and Deception in Everday Life*, edited by C. Saarni and M. Lewis. New York: Guilford Press, 1993.

Sanford, John. *Evil: The Shadow Side of Reality.* New York: Crossroads, 1981.

Schulman, Michael, and Eva Mekler. *Bringing Up a Moral Child.* 8th ed. Reading, Mass.: Addison-Wesley, 1985.

Schwartz, S. H. "Normative Influences on Altruism." In *Advances in Experimental Social Psychology*, edited by L. Berkowitz. New York: Academic Press, 1977.

Shaver, K. *The Attribution of Blame.* New York: Springer, 1985.

Shubik, Martin. "The Dollar Auction Game: A Paradox in Noncooperative Behavior and Escalation." *Journal of Conflict Resolution.* 1971, vol. 15.

Sigmon, Sandra, and C. R. Snyder. "Looking at Oneself in a Rose-Colored Mirror: The Role of Excuses in the Negotiation of a Personal Reality," edited by Michael Lewis and Carolyn Saarni. New York: Guilford Press, 1993.

Snyder, C. R. "Collaborative Companions: The Relationship of Self-Deception and Excuse-Making." In *Self-Deception and Understanding*, edited by M. Martin. Lawrence, Kan.: Regents Press of Kansas, 1985.

Snyder, C. R., R. L. Higgins, and R. J. Stucky. *Excuses: Masquerades in Search of Grace.* New York: Wiley-Interscience, 1983.

Staub, Ervin. "Helping a Distressed Person: Social, Personality, and Stimulus Determinants." In *Advances in Experiemental and Social Psychology*, vol. 7, edited by L. Berkowitz. New York: Academic Press, 1974.

——. *The Roots of Evil: The Origins of Genocide and Other Group Violence*. New York: Cambridge University Press, 1989.

Taylor, S. *Positive Illusions: Creative Self-Deception and the Healthy Mind*. New York: Basic Books, 1989.

Teger, Allan. *Too Much Invested to Quit*. New York: Pergamon Press, 1980.

Wallach, E., and L. Wallach. *Rethinking Goodness*. Albany, N.Y.: State University of New York Press, 1990.

Wechsler, H. *What's So Bad About Guilt?*. New York: Simon & Schuster, 1990.

Wispe, L. *The Psychology of Sympathy*. New York: Plenum, 1991.